Once Upon a *Diet*

WHY DIETING AND DATING HAVE MORE IN COMMON THAN YOU THINK,
and How to Break Up With the Bad Habits To Fix
Your Health and Your Heart

TONI MARINUCCI, MS, RDN

DEDICATION

To all the boys at school who teased me about my weight and to the men who didn't love me back, it's because of you I can lead by example and show people their weight doesn't determine their worth.

And to all of my clients who trusted me to help them heal their relationship with food and allowed me to write about them in this book, your courage inspires me to keep going.

Please note, all names have been changed to protect my clients' privacy.

SPECIAL THANKS TO MY

Writing coach: John Romaniello
Book editor: Blair Shiff
Family and friends for their outpouring support
Team of RD's and Interns
Teachers and Mentors
@Tips_With_Toni followers since day 1 and now
And to my current partner who continues to show me what it truly means to be loved

TABLE OF CONTENTS

INTRODUCTION

I was in elementary school when I first realized I was supposed to hate my body. I'm not sure what exactly made it click. It could have been the *Teen People* magazine covers I saw with article titles like, "How To Get Bikini Ready," or the then-new trend of obsessing and speculating about the growing celebrity romance between Britney & Justin, or my countless viewings of the movie Grease. The main message seemed to be: "Change everything about yourself for a person you don't know that well."

The messages coming my way certainly contributed, but the overt social programming was only half of the issue. There was also the direct feedback I was receiving from the people around me.

At school, I was already being teased about my weight. Unfortunately, my home life offered little-to-no refuge. At family dinners, my father gave me stern looks when I filled my plate with too much food, his disapproval evident in the narrowing of his eyes and the soft shake of his head. My grandmother was less subtle, puffing her cheeks out to make herself look "fat" anytime I reached for a second helping.

Slowly, I began to feel like my body should be like what I saw in magazines. But it wasn't, and it still isn't. It's my own. I know that *now*, but between the teasing at school, the criticism at home and everything the world was showing me from every direction, 9-year-old me had no shot at accepting herself.

My story is not unique. Aspects are probably fairly specific to my path, but my mindset and perspective are pretty common aspects of the experience of being a young woman growing up in Western culture, especially in America.

It's been this way for a long time, and, while it's getting better -- at least in that we're more aware of it now -- we still hear stories about people making choices to "improve" their bodies with outrageous diets and unrealistic exercise plans.

My thirst for answers ultimately led to my decision to go to school to study nutrition.

I remember thinking, "*This is perfect.* I'll learn how to lose weight, get the body I want and be in the ideal environment to find a husband." That wasn't the healthiest of decision making looking back.

Fast forward years later: I finished college, and, although I didn't find a husband (which we'll get to later), I certainly found my calling. I became the Registered Dietitian I always wanted to be, and, for the past eight years, I've been helping people create and follow nutrition plans which lead them to healthier, happier lives.

I didn't know it then, but in retrospect, it's obvious my personal nutrition pitfalls were correlated with my dating life. And, after working with thousands of clients, I noticed I wasn't alone. It was a pattern.

Just as my clients would jump from diet to diet, hoping each one would be "The One," I would jump from relationship to relationship hoping for the same thing. But we never questioned if that diet or person was truly good for us or was what we needed at the time.

And we'd repeat this, over and over again, never taking the time to assess how to produce a different outcome. Failing to realize the diet we were following was basically the same diet, just in a different book or the guy we were dating was basically the same guy from our past, just with a different name and face.

My goal is to help you see the patterns, too. It's not to protect you from heartbreak or disappointment. We need those feelings to tell us what we care about most. And without hurt, anger and frustration, we can't *really* understand the type of life we want to live. Instead, I will teach you how to use these experiences as feedback so you can create the diet of your dreams and break any restrictive cycles preventing your personal growth.

By the end of this book, I also want to detach two ideas for you.

SEPARATE YOUR BODY AND YOURSELF

First, your assessment of your body is different from your assessment of yourself. In an ideal world, I want to help you love everything about your body. Every curve, every muscle, every bump, every cellulite dimple, every little scar or stretch mark or so-called imperfection. It's what makes you, *you*.

I know that type of attitude adjustment is a lifelong pursuit. I suspect none of us ever truly finish that process. So while I want you to love your body, my job here isn't to convince you to adore every piece of it immediately. My role is to help you stop thinking your body is the entirety of what you have to offer the world. *Your body is the least interesting thing about you*. With that said, what we do to nourish and protect our bodies can help us feel good and can also turn into an opportunity to change the way we look at ourselves.

I want you to love yourself even on days you're not totally *in love* with every part of your body. And, I know, we can accomplish *that* in this book.

SEPARATE YOUR BODY AND ITS IMPACT ON YOUR LOVE LIFE

Second, I want to help you divorce the association between your body (and the imaginary worthiness it supposedly grants) and your perception of how it affects your suitability as a romantic partner.

As evidenced in my own story, (which we'll explore throughout the next several chapters) we've been culturally conditioned to draw parallels between dieting and dating--between our physical bodies and our romantic prospects.

That thought process needs to go. *Immediately.*

I know it's not as simple as saying, "OK, I love my body now. I'm ready to find someone who loves me for me," and expecting just thinking it into existence will change everything. I'm well aware of the realities of dating, conditioned attraction and all the various things that go into romance and courtship.

Finding someone you love and who loves you isn't about your body; but, we can acknowledge your body may be a factor in setting the stage for that character to enter the story of your life.

One of our goals here is to lessen it as a factor, and our *main* goal is to help you realize you don't need to have a smaller body to make it a smaller issue in your mind. You need to break the association between the two.

While we treat dieting the same way we treat dating, we must stop associating, relating and melding the two.

Throughout the rest of this book (and hopefully beyond), I'm going to give you the tools to do that.

When you start to use the tools I give you to change your body, you'll realize you want to change your body because you love it not because you hate it. And, you'll be making these changes for *you*. These adjustments will be long-lasting because you will have separated your body and your relationships.

We'll explore all the ways you can break the paradigms and patterns created and cultivated by Western society to determine exactly how *you* can address and modify *your* nutritional program in a way that's just right for *you* and the body *you* want. Throughout this exploration, we'll also address a number of ways those same habits and behaviors may show up in the way you approach relationships.

Our examination, along with the outline I'll give you, will help you shift many of those behaviors, moving *away* from the mindset that you *need* to be in a relationship or in pursuit of a relationship to be happy. Above all, you'll disassociate the belief your ideal partner is just on the other side of getting your ideal body.

I want to help you change all of these things because -- at any size, at any time and regardless of your relationship status -- *you deserve to be happy.*

You have taken the first step to read my book, which indicates you care about yourself. Even if it's just a small part, it's an important step. Deciding you deserve to make life choices that will help you now and in the future is the best investment you'll ever make.

The irony of all this is these practices, which are designed to help you find your perfect nutrition plan, may just be the thing to lead you, whether directly or at least indirectly, to your perfect partner.

CHAPTER 1

HOW I LOST MY INNOCENCE
AND FOUND INSECURITY

"The day we fret about the future is
the day we leave our childhood behind."

-*Patrick Rothfuss*, Author of "The Name of the Wind"

The first time I followed a workout program on my own, I was 9 years old. I'll never forget it. It was June 1999. I was spending the summer in Dunedin, Florida, a small city between Tampa and Clearwater almost entirely populated by grandparents who moved there to retire. My YiaYia and Papou were second-generation Greek Americans who moved south to avoid the brutal Northeast winters they braved as native New Yorkers.

That summer, just like every summer between the ages of 8 and 16, I flew down to visit them with my cousin, who was only a year older than me. The two of us hopped on a plane after an adult dropped us off.

Before I'd finished that school year, I knew I should prioritize changing the way I looked. What I knew, beyond all doubt, was my summer in Florida wasn't just about spending time by the pool with my family. It was about getting into shape, and that's just what I was going to do.

We had been in our grandparents' condo for about two weeks, which was long enough to settle in but not long enough to fully acclimate to how the humidity permeated everything. A faint musk always filled the room, which simply smelled like *Florida* to me -- the not-quite-mildewy scent of linen throw pillows that never quite dry out.

It was, however, plenty of time to have reprogrammed one of the preset stereo buttons in my Papou's Cadillac. We settled on 93.3, the closest thing to a Top 40s station to be found in that town. Radios blasted the smash hits of the day like Ricky Martin's "Livin' La Vida Loca," and Santana's "Smooth" featuring Matchbox 20's lead singer Rob Thomas.

The pop-music war raged between the Backstreet Boys and *NSYNC, and the battle lines were drawn in the ever-escalating Britney Spears/Christina Aguilera conflict. But even elementary-school me recognized those pop-feuds didn't seem to be equal. Instead, where the boy bands revolved around tight melodies and synchronized dance moves, the divas seemed to be all about whose outfit was the tightest or revealed the most.

Even though I noticed the difference, I didn't realize how it was directly influencing me. The outside world was telling me if I looked like models and celebrities, I would be more accepted, liked and, eventually, loved. I'd received the message loud and clear. This made me want to make a change. The metamorphosis I was hoping for would be designed to make me, Toni Marinucci, worthy of acceptance in the world.

It was in the guest room of that damp Dunedin condo I committed to losing the weight, to fixing[1] my body, to do whatever was necessary to make Backstreet Boy Kevin Richardson--or anyone else, for that matter--fall in love with

---

[1] To fix something, means something is broken, but there was nothing wrong with my body. Yet, after being teased for being bigger than my peers, for looking different, I didn't see it that way.

me. If I wanted to get everything I ever wanted, I needed to look like someone Kevin Richardson would date. And, in my mind, the path to looking like a pop star was to exercise for hours.

That day, I put on my lime green short shorts, tied a knot on the side of my white tank top and laced up my sneakers. I adjusted the pink scrunchie holding my obnoxiously high ponytail back. And then, I added the pièce de résistance: The white Nike sweatband I'd brought with me from New York to keep my bangs (which I hated but my mother forced me to keep) out of my face.

Looking in the mirror, I knew I was ready. I was going to do it. I *needed* to do this. I felt like a badass. No. I *was* a badass.

It was at that moment, 9-year-old, badass Toni took what she thought was the first step toward a lifetime of good health, fitness, success, joy and, eventually, love. So, I popped *Barbie's Dance Workout* in the VCR, because that, as we all know, is how badasses workout.

Looking back now, that once motivating Barbie workout tape was also a first step toward a dangerous paradigm in which your self-worth is tied to your weight.

Anyway, my first workout went well. Dancing around in that guest room was fun. My exercise area was limited to the 5-foot-by-5-foot space between the two twin beds my cousin and I slept in. Barbie's voice sounded thin and tinny from the speakers on the 14-inch box TV, but I didn't care. It was exhilarating.

I loved the way the sweat felt dripping down my face and how sore I was the next day. I finally felt productive.

But, by my fifth workout, things were less fun. I thought I'd be as thin as my classmates by now. Sure, my dancing was getting better, but my body wasn't progressing as quickly as I had hoped. In fact, I felt like it was getting worse. I was more aware of it now. I didn't like the way my legs looked as I danced in the mirror or how my belly jiggled as I jumped up and down.

These feelings stayed with me long after the workout was finished. I couldn't move without being aware of my body. I noticed the way the light refracted in the pool water and made my limbs look bloated. I felt it when my skin bulged over the car's seat belt. I saw it when I looked down at my lumpy-looking shadow on the sidewalk. It was everywhere. I was everywhere. I couldn't escape it.

It wasn't long before what was fun and freeing turned into obligation and punishment.

Don't get me wrong, dancing was enjoyable, but enjoying it wasn't my motivation. And, eventually, dance wasn't the only workout I chose because, somehow, it didn't feel like it was enough. I had a lot to prove to myself, to my family, to Kevin Richardson, to *everyone*.

So, I'd run around the condo complex and swim laps in the community pool before feeling like I earned my relaxation time.

The pride I used to feel after a workout faded. It didn't matter how much I didn't *want* to work out, I felt an immense amount of pressure like I *had* to work out. Eventually, my mind was wired to believe: "If I exercise, I'll lose weight, stop getting teased and *then* my crush will like me."

Believe it or not, the exercise part was easy. That I could control. But what and how much I ate? *That* was the hard part.

Food was constantly on my mind. I loved it. As I'd eat my toast with butter, I'd be so excited to eat the next one with jam, and the following with cream cheese, and then one more with jam *and* cream cheese.

Immediately after breakfast, I'd start thinking about what we were going to have for lunch and couldn't wait to hear what restaurant we'd be going to for dinner, secretly hoping it was somewhere I could get my favorite dish: Disco fries. What are disco fries? Well, they're french fries but covered with melted mozzarella cheese and gravy. Seeing a trend here?[2]

There was mixed messaging everywhere. We were allowed to have dessert despite the comments of "watch what you eat" throughout the day. By the time my grandparents passed out the ice cream, I felt conflicted. I wasn't sure if saying yes was giving into the temptation because I knew it would be served with a side of guilt and shame. But saying no to it could lead to praise and pride. I'd often choose to not have it and wait to eat it in secret when I could enjoy it without being judged.

My cousin and I would wait for them to go to bed, and then sneak our way into the kitchen, trying not to make a sound, which was hard. If you haven't noticed, almost all "junk food" comes in a crinkly wrapper, as if you're supposed to notify the world and feel immediate shame for eating it.

We made it from the guest room to the kitchen and back without ever getting caught. It was exhilarating to eat these treats without being watched.

---

[2] I was exhibiting signs of overindulging, which we'll address how I learned to manage this in later chapters.

Every summer when I came back from Florida, my parents would say "You look good. It looks like you've lost weight." I'm not going to lie, hearing that felt *good*. I thought I looked thinner. It was the perfect confidence boost I needed to walk into school again.

But every new year, I'd walk into school and still get teased for my weight. In the fifth grade, it was for my Halloween costume when I decided to dress up as a blue M&M. Apparently, I didn't need to wear an oversized suit to "look that wide." According to the boys in my class, I could've just worn a T-shirt.

In sixth grade, after begging for what seemed like ever, my parents finally got my sister and me a computer. Immediately, I created an AOL account. I was so excited. All of my friends talked about Instant Messenger, their screen names and fun chat rooms. I thought this was going to be the best thing in life. At that time in the world, being in constant contact with friends was new and thrilling. Few things were as invigorating as the chiming sound of an Instant Message (IM).

But this excitement died when I got a message from a username I didn't recognize. Four words flashed across my screen. First was -- excuse my language -- "fat fuck," followed by "you're disgusting." What came after that was every other cruel comment an 11-year-old boy could hurl at someone. I'd aggressively type back the only response I learned to defend myself: "Sticks and stones may break my bones, but words can never hurt me!"

But they did hurt me. A lot. Especially because I found out later those IMs came from a classmate who sat behind me in my homeroom. A boy who I thought might actually like me. *Clearly, my radar was way off.*

I have a story similar to that every new school year.

I got so used to hearing I was overweight, I started talking to myself the same way everyone else did. It even found its way into my homework. In the eighth grade, I wrote a poem for Mrs. Johnson's English class in which I talked about how I hated the way my body looked and so desperately wanted it to change, as if bemoaning it would solve all of my problems.[3]

It didn't go unnoticed. Mrs. Johnson gave me an A+ with a side of *"Please See Me"* and sent me straight to the guidance counselors office. But it also didn't solve my problems.

Eventually, the teasing, media imagery and well-intentioned but ultimately damaging commentary from my family wore me down.

I remember feeling a crushing shift in me. Suddenly, this joyful, light-hearted kid who never used to care what other people thought was gone. In her place was someone new: A nervous pre-teen increasingly overwhelmed by thoughts that her looks dictated her overall likability.

This little girl, like so many generations before her, was conditioned to believe if she looked better, life would be better.

From that moment on, I remember obsessing over two things. No. 1: Looking like the thin women in magazines, and No. 2: Getting the boy I was crushing on to like me back. The less popular I was with the boys, the more I blamed my weight. As I got older, that connection deepened.

---

[3] For the record, I tried hard to find this poem, but couldn't. Maybe it's sitting in my parents' basement or maybe I threw it away to cast it from my memory. Either way, tossing it out didn't dent the impact it made on me.

Through all those years, I learned important lessons I wanted to impart on others to help them. That's why I chose to study nutrition.

In working with hundreds of women over the years, I discovered they learned to hate their bodies during their childhood, too. Sometimes they learned it directly by being told they needed to lose weight if they wanted a shot at making the dance team. Other times, they learned it indirectly, when their younger, thinner and more popular sister got asked to go to prom, and they didn't.

As a result, they spent their entire lives trying to love their bodies more by changing them. But after decades of trying to do the same thing, I'm here to assure you the path to loving your body doesn't come from changing it or shrinking it or "toning" it.

It comes from understanding it, respecting it and treating it like you love it, even if you don't quite yet. Taking care of our bodies may mean adjusting what we eat, which often will change the way we *look*, but if we truly want to *feel* better, by having more energy, strength and confidence (regardless of our size), we must first change the way we *think*.

The truth is: None of us are broken. Our bodies are unique to us, and that's what makes them beautiful.

It's also worth noting that, for many, part of the journey to self love involves weight loss, and that's OK. Weight loss is a perfectly acceptable goal, and, for some, it's an important step toward overall better health. However, *it cannot be your only goal.* The important thing is to avoid sacrificing your mental health in order to achieve that goal and to instead truly understand the *why* behind it.

Are you doing it for you or for someone else? For example, are you trying to prove to your ex they made a mistake by breaking up with you and you believe shrinking your way into a size 4 pant size will make them see that?

This is why I created *The Once Upon a Diet Method*, and it's what makes it so special. It allows you to improve your health in a way that makes sense for *you*. You don't tailor yourself to the diet you found on Google. You form the method on your own.

My book is an outline to a guide that will help you create your own path. Instead of locking outside yourself for answers, *The Once Upon A Diet Method* will give you the tools to look inward in order to figure out what you need for yourself.

It will help you follow through on your decisions and teach you to pivot when necessary. That's what really matters: Not jumping from diet to diet, hoping to stumble on the right one. And it's most certainly *not* gritting your teeth and forcing yourself to stick to something that clearly isn't a good fit for you.

Unlike Cinderella's step sisters who tried jamming their feet into whatever slipper came along, even when it clearly wasn't a good fit, *The Once Upon a Diet Method* is the opposite of that. It's the key to unlocking your inner Goldilocks, giving you all the tools to make sure the plan you create for yourself is *just right*. And it will be because it's just for you.

CHAPTER 2

CINDERELLA AND
THE NOT-SO-HAPPY ENDING

"Your diet is not only what you eat. It's what you watch, what you listen to, what you read, and the people you hang around … "

- Unknown

When I was in middle school, I remember sitting in salon waiting areas, flipping through magazines until my mom was done with her monthly pampering session: Acrylic nails, hair coloring followed by a wash and blow out.

I'd look at the pretty hair models, admiring the fancy wedding dresses and imagine how I'd look in snow white. I hoped one day I'd be able to lose enough weight to be able to wear one[4] of those myself. Even in my daydreams, I envisioned myself thinner. I was sure when I lost weight, I'd be worthy of love. I'd be complete and happy when I found my Prince Charming.

One month, Britney Spears was featured on the cover of *Teen People* since she had recently danced around in a risque belly shirt for a Pepsi commercial. Next to her and all the other airbrushed celebrities who rocked outfits the average person wouldn't dare to wear in public were headlines for *"Hot Lips,"* *"Best Bikini Styles" and "How To Find Love."*

---

[4] Note: There weren't many "plus-size" models back then.

You didn't even have to *open* the magazine to be influenced by the repetitive messaging: The better you look, the more suitable you are for love and marriage.

Like millions of girls sitting in thousands of salons flipping through those same pages, I was unknowingly programming my brain to hate my body.

But I didn't learn that only from magazines. From the time we are old enough to have stories read to us, our sponge-like baby brains start soaking up a theme: The more conventionally attractive you are, the easier, better and happier you'll be.

In so many fairy tales, the princesses are the same shape: Hourglass figures with tiny, tiny waists. You saw their size and knew they'd find love and have a happy ending. What you never saw was plus-size girls getting the guy.

You almost wonder if they didn't get the guy because they didn't put themselves out there due to fear of rejection or if they've been rejected so many times because of their size, they just gave up. We'll never know for sure since they rarely were featured or given non-villain roles.

As we got older, dating apps made this even worse. Since the majority of apps are based on aesthetics and gut reactions to pictures, women stress they won't match with someone because they're in a bigger body. Or worse, they fear meeting up with the person they connect with and worry their date will be upset their photo from a year ago doesn't reflect how they look now.

Charlie came to me for weight loss, knowing this time she

wanted to do it in a sustainable way. But like so many of my clients, the issues ran deeper than getting to a lower number on the scale. We had to work through that together.

She was looking for a method that wouldn't require rigid rules or giving up her favorite foods and rob her of time with her two precious daughters and loving husband.

We'd been working on incorporating the foundational principles I begin teaching all of my clients at the outset of their program:

- Implementing a balanced breakfast
- Committing to at least 10 minutes of intentional movement daily
- Drinking more water
- Adding more vegetables
- Going to bed around the same time each night

These seemingly small behaviors are the first steps to forming long-term habits and achieving significant changes.

A month into the process, Charlie was feeling pretty good. She'd lost a few pounds but also found her energy had increased, as had her libido. Her skin was smoother, her joints were less achy, and she was now having regular bowel movements.

Outwardly, Charlie's clothes were fitting better, which made her feel more comfortable in them and more confident without them. After her 30-day check in, Charlie told me she felt in charge of her body and, for the first time, was convinced this was going to be the way she would lose the weight *for good*.

Two days later, Charlie encountered her first real-world challenge: An upcoming social gathering.

Here's exactly what she told me: *"I was invited out to the lake with some new friends today. Definitely a little anxious about being in a bathing suit around others."*

Just 48 hours prior to that, Charlie had been sharing with me how great she felt, but her mentality quickly shifted when she was expected to publicly expose parts of her body she had intentionally kept hidden for years. The proud, optimistic woman was now feeling discouraged and ashamed because, despite her valiant efforts, her body would never measure up to the bodies of her naturally petite friends.

Understanding her anxiety, I suggested we hop on a call to talk it out. We used *The Once Upon A Diet Method* to work through the experience. I'll go into greater detail later on the step-by-step, but what's important here is Charlie's initial thought process.

The real issue is on the inside: Charlie's perception of her appearance. As we've covered already, all women experience this. At that moment, Charlie wasn't able to step outside from her own judgment of her body, let alone other people's thoughts, while simultaneously unraveling a lifetime's worth of societal programming. That takes time. Lots of it.

To help her, we started from the *outside*. I asked her what she thought her options were for handling the situation. Her answers were revealing.

Avoidance was the first, as it often is. "I could just not go," she said. After a brief back-and-forth about what that would mean, she set it aside. The outing on the lake was a chance to deepen her connection with her new friends, and that was important to her.

I asked her to tell me about a time when her feelings about her body had kept her from doing something. Charlie rattled off a list of beach days she didn't go to, parties she didn't attend and even a wedding she'd skipped.

Then, I asked her to tell me about a time when her feelings about her body had *almost* kept her from doing something, but she went anyway. Charlie took a few minutes to think. She stayed silent for so long I thought our connection was lost, until finally she brightened when she thought of her husband. "My first date with Jeff," she recalled.

Charlie's experience of feeling embarrassed of her body wasn't a new one to her. Fearful of rejection because she couldn't fit into the size 6 skinny jeans she'd worn in high school, she stayed single for years, telling herself she needed to lose weight before she could try to date.

Fortunately, on the fateful night of her and Jeff's first date, Charlie's aversion to being rude and canceling at the last minute overruled her fear of being judged, and she decided not to ghost Jeff, "the hot lawyer from Match." Charlie realized if she kept trying to lose weight for an event, she would keep missing out on life. And it's a good thing she didn't ditch her date because she may have never found the happy marriage she has now.

With that memory firmly in her mind, Charlie decided skipping the lake wasn't going to get her what she wanted, so we moved to other options.

She could cover herself up, she thought, but then she

remembered covering up just drew *more attention.* The idea of wearing something more modest also caused some resentment. Charlie revealed she was always the only one who wore shorts over her bathing suit, dressed in oversized T-shirts and wrapped a towel around her waist to hide her rolls when she'd sit.

Throughout her life, a pattern had emerged. In any social gathering at which revealing attire was appropriate, Charlie would cover up, find a spot and stay there while watching everyone else jump freely off diving boards, swim and *run* around, not even slightly concerned their bellies would jiggle as they did.

We talked through it some more, and she realized that while covering up "solves" the problem of people not seeing her body, it wouldn't solve her problem with being seen in general. It could make connecting with her new friends more difficult and that couldn't be the answer.

Over the course of our 35-minute conversation, Charlie listed and discarded a few other options, like staying beneath the water's surface all day so as not to be seen or having a few extra drinks until liquid courage kicked in.

In the end, we settled on the only true option there ever really was: Charlie was to go to the lake in a bathing suit which she felt the most confident in (or at least not insecure, which is how these things usually start), and use it as an opportunity to work through the discomfort.

A week later, Charlie went to the lake. And as you might expect, she had a great time. As it turned out, no one stared at her. There were no snarky comments. In fact, everyone told her how much they loved her swimsuit. More than that, they told her how happy they were that she'd come and how much they enjoyed spending time with her.

Most people don't care what you look like. They care about *who you are* and how you treat them. Sometimes it helps to be reminded of that.

That day on the lake set a new reference point and shifted the conversation for Charlie.

Her story is like so many others, both in terms of her self-doubts and how she worked to overcome them.

I wish someone would've been around to teach that lesson to 12-year-old Toni as she flipped through those fashion magazines. It could have saved her a lot of time and heartache.

Starting with those tabloid-laden afternoons waiting for my mom to finish at the salon and continuing well into my young adulthood, everything from health and fitness magazines to gossip websites reaffirmed what I'd learned from fairy tales.

At no point did I concern myself with thoughts of *health*. I was solely fixated on losing the weight. I assumed changing my body was the key to a successful social life and an essential ingredient in my romantic future.

Naturally, the mental connection I made between my body and my happiness deepened. This led to multiple failed attempts to achieve the perfect body with the hope to feel *ready* enough to put myself out there. We often have the same attitude, impatience and even urgency to feel comfortable in our own skin as we do to find love. Until we break that connection, we'll just keep failing.

You see, we date the same way we diet.

CHAPTER 3

JUST BECAUSE IT'S 'WORKING' DOESN'T MEAN IT WORKS

"Some people believe holding on and hanging in there are signs of great strength. However, there are times when it takes more strength to know when to let go and then do it."

- *Ann Landers,* American advice columnist

We treat dating the same way we treat dieting. We're so fixated on the end result, we forget that, in order to continue enjoying those results, we have to keep putting in effort every day.

I believe there are two types of people in this world: Bouncers and Planters. Both of these types want to figure out the result as fast as possible but don't realize that taking the time to learn from the process is actually going to help them get there faster. While their attitudes are similar, their approaches to it are different.

Bouncers jump but never land. They go from diet to diet or relationship to relationship, try things for a bit and declare it "doesn't work" before ever really giving it a chance. They forget the really bad dates or rough experiences *are* what helps them find what works for them.

Then, there are Planters. Planters also bounce but not for long. So hopeful for a home, they latch on to when something feels halfway decent and land. But instead of leaving when things go south, they come up with multiple excuses and give the situation *way* too many chances. They know how much energy goes into finding a new home, so once their roots are solidified, they're hesitant to try again.

Sometimes, we dive into a diet (or a relationship), without really thinking things through. We get so caught up in the honeymoon phase when we feel the initial shift, we don't acknowledge if what made us feel that way is what we want to spend the rest of our lives with.

We all know why that's happening. You've added in more fruits and vegetables and you're drinking more water. In short, you're taking better care of yourself and becoming more aware of what you're doing, so your body is doing what bodies do. For a while, atleast.

Then, the predictable slowdown comes around, and things aren't so bright and shiny anymore. We suddenly question if the work we're putting in is beneficial. This is the turning point for so many.

For Planters, the answer is always patience. "Stay the course! Keep doing what you're doing! It's not working as well? Do more! Work harder!"

But for the Bouncers, a slowdown in progress means giving up and looking for the next shiny object. "If it's not working, then it's not worth holding on to, but something will be, eventually. The answer is out there somewhere! Get out there, and find it!"

Presented so simply, it's easy to see why neither of these methods are particularly effective approaches to something as complex as relationships.

The Planter means well, and there's a lot to be said for persistence, but patience taken to the extreme looks a lot like ignoring the red flags.

The Bouncer is doing their best by trying to move forward at all times because they want to *know* what they're doing is working.

When it comes to addressing our nutrition, we need to take some advice from the Planters and some advice from the Bouncers.

The perseverance Planters display is necessary for long-term success, but being unwilling to shift when needed will repeatedly lead to a dead-end. Bouncers' radar for when things are off is useful, but what they need to learn is not everything is going to be perfect.

With nutrition, the way to progress is to remind yourself you're working through a *process*, because a *process* can be and should be adjusted when needed. But to do that, you need to know you're on the right plan for *you*--one that *will* work in the long run, one designed with built-in flexibility.[5]

I'm a Planter. I'm someone who tries too hard for too long, convinced waiting a little longer will bring something back to life. For the longest time, I thought I was so different from Bouncers, but after writing this book, I see how the two kinds overlap.

Both just want to feel good, desired and secure.

---

[5] Relationships, as we'll discuss later, are the same, no matter how right someone is for you. There will be issues, arguments along with ups-and-downs. People change and grow while revealing more of themselves. Minor incompatibilities arise. A Bouncer who panics the moment the sizzle starts to cool and lives life in search of the "eternal honeymoon feeling" isn't likely to form a lasting relationship. The Planter who pretends everything is fine when all the evidence points to change being necessary may have a relationship that lasts, but may not be a happy or healthy one at that.

WHEN 'NOTHING'S WRONG' DOESN'T MEAN ANYTHING'S RIGHT

I'll never forget my first week of college. I was eager to learn and excited for a fresh start.

My battle with my weight was a constant concern during high school. My workouts, which had evolved from *Barbie's Dance Party* to marathon elliptical sessions, hadn't changed my body, my situation or my relationship status. I'd gone through school feeling less like Cinderella and more like the pre-carriage pumpkin since there was still no prince in sight.

Now enrolled as a Dietetics major, I was absolutely positive studying nutrition was going to be the thing that changed that pattern.

I was going to learn about food and energy balance. Most importantly, I'd find out the secret, precious knowledge I hadn't discovered in magazines or books yet. I wanted to identify the diet that would bibbidi-bobbidi-boo me into the person I was *supposed to be.*

Which is *sort of* what happened. Or, at least, that's what I thought. I was so certain that I convinced myself I had found it on the very first day of class.

Eager to learn, I arrived early, making sure I'd get a seat in the front row. I opened my notebook, put my pen in my hand and glued my eyes to the whiteboard, impatiently waiting for the lecture to begin. Minutes passed like hours as I nervously shook my leg. The anticipation was killing me.

My professor started teaching us about the benefits of vegetarianism. That's when I had my first "ah-ha" moment.

Immediately, my ears perked up, I felt my belly sink into my stomach, and I thought, "This is it. This is how I'm finally going to lose the weight."

And just like that, I decided I was a vegetarian. By the end of the class, I was absolutely convinced this was not only the right diet for me, but it was the *only* diet for me. I had determined *not* being a vegetarian up until that point had been my problem all along.

Needless to say, I couldn't wait to get to the dining hall for lunch, to try my first meatless meal.

But before lunch, I had another class on my schedule: A physical education class called Introduction to Weight Training. This was also part of my master plan. I figured signing up for a gym class would be an easy A and another way to help me lose some weight.

Confident I'd already discovered the secret to changing my life, I was looking forward to adding exercise into the mix. This was going to be great.

And it was. As I was working out, I had a feeling someone was looking at me. I spotted the source: Side glances and conversation exchanged between two tall, muscular men. I didn't think much of it, considering this was something I was accustomed to at this point. Being the chubby girl in the gym was always bound to draw attention.

My experience up until that point had been all negative. I had a general awareness I was being judged, if not outright mocked. To offset this, I'd taken to hiding my body with baggy sweatshirts. But that was *High School* Toni. *College* Toni had ditched the sweatshirt for tight leggings and a tank top. Well, technically, *two* tank tops, as the double layer would disguise my midsection, which protruded more than I believed was acceptable.

Somewhat self-conscious, I glanced over at the two guys, and then looked away. They were *definitely* looking at me and talking about me, but it seemed different. Was I being checked out? I'd seen it in movies before, but I had never experienced it in real life. The thought of that made me smile and blush, which was, evidently, an invitation. One of the guys, also smiling, made his way over to me and introduced himself. I wasn't just being checked out. I was actively being *flirted* with. And here I was, in the gym, flirting back and having a great conversation. Five minutes later, I'd given him my number.

"Being a vegetarian is amazing," I thought. *"I haven't even eaten anything yet, and it's already working."*

After our class, he escorted me to lunch, and I had my first vegetarian meal: A meatless lasagna that would've horrified my Italian family. In truth, it wasn't very good, but I certainly didn't care. My life was obviously on the right track.

Lunch led to walking to class together, and, after a few casual "hangouts" (which I learned was what people in 2008 said instead of *dates*), he became my boyfriend.

College Toni was *killing it*. Less than a week in, I had gotten my diet figured out, my future on track and a boyfriend by my side. It felt like the rest of my life had just started.

Now, this is where the Cinderella story ends and where real life begins. Spoiler alert, we did *not* get married.

We dated for nearly three years, and it was a good relationship. It wasn't until much later I realized how great it had been for me that it was a *good* relationship. Not good as in the opposite of bad, but good as in several steps up from *meh*. The problem was it was also much further away from *amazing*.

This is something almost all Planters are guilty of, but nearly everyone needs to learn.

A few separate issues caused our breakup. We could have worked through them. We could have made it work or, at least, made it *workable*. We had good communication, respect and understanding of each other's wants and were ready to support each other's dreams. It would've been *fine*.

But *fine* isn't, and shouldn't be, the goal for anyone. Something was missing.

Months after it ended, a beautiful realization changed the way I looked at nearly everything in my life: Just because it *works*, doesn't mean it's working. He was a great guy, but he just wasn't *the* guy for me.

I didn't want to live a *fine* life; I wanted to live a genuinely happy one.

Looking back on College Toni, who was so eager to jump into whatever seemed to fit the mold she'd created and so desperate to be loved and accepted, it's almost shocking she was able to walk away from something that was *fine*. Especially when I look at how many times I've had to learn that lesson when it came to dieting.

Just as I'd done with my boyfriend, I jumped into the first

nutritional relationship that presented itself.

Being a vegetarian was great at first. I had a ton of energy, I felt like I had some kind of structure with food choices and it was easier to turn down unhealthy options simply because there was meat in them.[6] Moreover, I did lose 10 pounds and kept it off. Between being a vegetarian and weight training, my body composition had changed a bit.

Everyone respected my decision and was supportive. But eventually, being veggie *really wasn't* working for me. I was constantly hungry, bored of eating the same thing daily and felt bloated all the time.

But, like a good Planter, I stuck with it. It *had* worked. Did I really want to go back to where I was before and regain the weight? The same justifications I'd used to stay in the relationship I knew wasn't right for me surfaced again, now in *this* aspect of my life.

It wasn't as easy for me to let go of my nutritional habits, though.

Many of my clients have come to me with this same mentality. Having lost weight on low-carb diets, rigid meal plans and programs requiring meal-replacement shakes and bars, they felt trapped.

They'd start something new--celery juice, keto, paleo, sometimes even a combo of a few--but before long, they found their enthusiasm waning. What once felt good began

---

[6] One of the more interesting things I learned is people are automatically more supportive of your food choices as a vegetarian than they are when you say you're on a diet. It's a lot less common for someone to urge a vegetarian to have just one bite of a hamburger than it is for them to try to convince you to have a cookie on a low-carb diet.

to feel boring. They'd stick with it, going through the motions until their experience with the diet shifted from *acceptable* to *intolerable*.

This is a crossroads for so many. Whatever you choose, you feel cornered.

Many of my clients fear they'll backslide. They believe saying goodbye to powdered protein and juice cleanses meant saying "hello, again" to the 10 pounds they'd lost while starving themselves into a body they once hated.

And they weren't wrong. In a meta-analysis done by NIH of 29 long-term weight loss studies, more than half of the lost weight was regained within two years, and by five years, more than 80 percent of lost weight was regained.

So, some people choose to cling to what seemingly worked, remain miserable and complain of the lack of variety, low energy and tasteless meals. But most people decide to flee, so desperate to feel unburdened only to be reminded shortly thereafter they actually didn't know how to be free in the first place. We're conditioned from a young age to diet to get the body we want, but so many of us are not taught how to simply eat properly.

My client Alexa described this as "feeling like a slave to the diet." She couldn't see a way out without "ruining everything she'd worked for."

Without having something to follow, without a list of "good" vs. "bad" foods, she didn't even know what to eat. Overwhelmed by conflicting information, Alexa felt guilty while eating just about any food. For every positive message, there was a negative one.

- An apple a day keeps the doctor away. Oh, wait, no. Fruit has too much sugar. You have to avoid it.
- Milk is a great source of protein and builds strong bones. Just kidding, dairy is ruining your digestive system.
- Meat is bad for you, unless you're doing keto, in which case, it's the best. But keto is bad. Or is it good?
- And what about eggs? Are you supposed to eat the yolks? In the time since you read this sentence, eggs have gone from being healthy to unhealthy and back again at least twice.
- Vegetables are universally healthy. But only if they're organic, of course.

We'll come back to all of these conflicting messages later--including how to navigate them. The point is, Alexa isn't alone.

Alexa grew up with a refrigerator filled with SlimFast, watching her mom skip breakfast, lunch and occasionally dinner. At 12 years old, she was forced to go to Weight Watchers meetings after her doctors said her BMI was too high. A few years later, she was sent to a nutritionist who instructed her to cut out the foods she loved.

By the time she was in her 30s, Alexa had lost and regained the same 25 pounds at least 25 times. Each time, it seemed to come off slower and slower and come back on more quickly. By the time we started to work together, her anxiety about "needing" to change her body was matched only by her fear of eventually regaining whatever weight she managed to lose. She had become a Bouncer.

Still, she kept going up and down, moving through life, jumping from one trend to the next, never feeling free or in control. To use her words, she felt "stuck in the chains" of her yo-yo dieting, but she just didn't know any other way to function.

Alexa wasn't just struggling with this pattern in the nutrition department. She was feeling the same way in her dating life.

All of her friends had boyfriends, and she felt pressured to have one, too. She was tired of being the third wheel. She feared pretty soon her friends would get married, would move into a big suburban house and be too busy having and taking care of babies and bonding with other moms and moms-to-be than to make time for her.

Rather than recognizing those lifestyle choices weren't something Alexa currently wanted for herself, her family and friends assumed it was because she hadn't found the right guy yet. Thus, there was an unspoken open invitation for her to be set up on a date with any single man her brother, mother, best friend or co-worker knew.

Instead of questioning if she even wanted the same things they had, she went along with it. She was constantly being set up on dates with "eligible" bachelors, whose only prerequisite seemed to be a man who was old enough for marriage. Alexa was almost never asked what type of guy she was looking for and was, instead, sent men who were rarely described as funny, respectful, kind or sweet. (More on this ever-present trend in the next chapter.)

As a result, she bounced from relationship to relationship like she did with diets, enjoying the honeymoon phase when sparks flew, but always leaving once she realized not all that glitters is gold.

It's not that she didn't eventually want what her friends had, but she needed to do it on her own terms. But, just like society had forced her into diets, she felt pushed to date.

That's when I told Alexa she had to speak up. Letting others tell her what to do, being dragged to Weight Watchers with her mom and to a nutritionist with her dad, didn't end in childhood. Years into her adulthood, when her friends asked her to follow some crazy meal plan promoted by an Instagram influencer, she'd join them. She needed to set hard boundaries.

But after a few months of us working together, this changed. We identified a few patterns that needed addressing if she wanted to feel in charge of her diet. To help her stop overeating and lose the amount of weight *she wanted*, one of the goals we came up with was sticking to three, balanced meals per day. Prior to working with me, she never ate breakfast thinking this was the healthy thing to do because Intermittent Fasting was trendy. We identified that skipping breakfast led her to overeat in the evening.

A simple intervention of encouraging her to eat *something* to rev up her metabolism before 10 a.m. was enough to get her adjusted to a new eating schedule. This encouraged hunger, a normal physiological response in which diet culture has made us believe is wrong to satisfy. Once you start to listen to your hunger cues, you honor your hunger cues. By honoring her hunger cues during the day, she was able to slow down her decision-making process in the evenings and choose a dinner before her eyes became bigger than her stomach.

After a few weeks of eating more consistently throughout the day, she found her cravings for things like sweets, salt and fried foods reduced significantly. She began craving healthier options, paying more attention to her hunger cues and noticed she hadn't overeaten in weeks. She felt great.

Then came a big test. Her friend asked her to fast with her. She realized a fast would only force her to backslide after all the progress she has made and offset her mood and energy which has significantly improved.

She respectfully declined her friend's request to fast with her, promised to morally support her friend instead and felt really good about it. Now, she just needed to apply the same lesson to her dating life, and she would continue to feel like she was living *her* life.

♥ ♥ ♥

I was a vegetarian for five years. It only took two for me to realize it wasn't right for me, but the next three years were spent trying to *make it work,* no matter what.

Not only was it making my life more difficult (intestinal stress, food choices, etc.), it had stopped "working." I hadn't lost weight in months, and I wasn't as happy with my body as I wanted to be.

So, I did the logical thing: *I made it harder!* I went from vegetarian to vegan. My food choices were reduced by at least 80%. My weight went unchanged, and my bloating got worse.

Seems like a good time to stop, right? Nope. I made it more complicated *again,* going gluten free on top of it all. Once again, I reduced the total number of foods I was "allowed" to eat. Eating had transitioned from a boring chore to an exercise in self-punishment.

There was a similar parallel to my romantic life, too.

After I ended my first relationship, I stayed single for a couple years with zero interest in getting into a relationship with anyone new.

Fast forward two years, and I ended up in another long-term relationship that started out great but took a turn a few months in. It took an extreme situation to break us up before I realized he wasn't good for me, and I was holding onto the first three months we were together. I wish I could say I learned my lesson from that relationship, but I didn't. See? Self-punishing behavior again.

I knew I needed to start going about things differently.

Rather than just "taking time off from dating," I needed to *think about what I was learning.*

I'd already made this change in my nutritional life, I just needed to incorporate it in this aspect, too.

Like so many people, I learned the hard way that magazine articles titled "5 Days To Burn The Belly Fat" didn't hold the secret answer.

I also learned extreme restriction wasn't the solution either. It was part of the problem. Eating a cookie wasn't the issue. The issue was eating the *entire box* of cookies after no longer being able to ignore what my stomach was screaming at me.

It wasn't until I stopped looking outward and started looking inward I was able to find the balance in my eating habits. If I truly wanted to lose weight, gain confidence and feel comfortable in my skin, I needed to stop paying attention to how certain foods might make me look and start paying more attention to how they made me feel.

Using that as my guide, and after lots of trial and error, I created the best diet that worked for me for a lifetime.

Like finding the perfect mate, creating the best diet that works for you takes patience, an understanding there are no shortcuts to long-term change and, most importantly, *introspection.*

The first step on that journey is self-assessment, starting with a list of short but powerful questions.

In the following chapters, I will elaborate on these more, but to get you thinking, here they are:

1. **Will this last past the honeymoon phase?**
2. **Do you even *like* this?**
3. **What lessons did you learn from this?**

CHAPTER 4

WHY WE DIET HOW WE DATE
(AND HOW TO STOP SETTLING IN BOTH)

"You always deserve more than crumbs.
Don't settle for a fantasy or half-assed relationship."

- *Natalie Lue,* relationship advice blogger

My college relationship taught me a lot, and even though the breakup was painful, it was necessary. Or, at least, it seemed like the right move for my growth. Still, there were some glaring gaps in my romantic education which became clearer over time.

One of those much-needed lessons was how long you're "allowed" to process a breakup. About four months after my nearly-three-year relationship ended, it seemed as though the entire world had held a meeting and collectively decided my allotted mourning time had expired.

Encouraged by nearly everyone around me, it became clear I'd been single long enough, and it was time to *get back out there.*

It wasn't until I did indeed get back out there and started to date I became aware of another gap in my education: I never learned how to date.

Sure, I knew how to dress up, go on dates and hold a conversation, but, I didn't really understand what I was supposed to be looking for.

I don't think dating should be quite like an *interview* process, but there should, at least, be a general assessment of chemistry and shared values.

The thing is, I didn't know that yet. I treated every date as a prelude to a potential relationship instead of seeing if we were compatible enough to get to that point. I had absolutely no idea how to be selective. *Any* kind of validation or attention was so appealing, I didn't stop to consider the source of it or the intention behind it.

Even when I knew the guy was emotionally unavailable, my mind went to "Well, one day, he will be." Rather than taking that as a sign to move on and date someone else, I thought I could fix him and turn him into my Prince Charming. But guess what? He never did. I was constantly disappointed because no guy could measure up to this fantasy I had in my mind.

This led me to "taking time off" from being in a relationship, which lasted about three years.

I was either totally closed off to meeting someone and didn't date, or I met someone, had some *semblance* of a connection and immediately jumped into a relationship with them. When I did dive into those relationships, my entire life was usually affected by it and, to some degree, rearranged to support it.

Even though it looked like a new guy and a new relationship, it was the same, old story. But because I was so hooked on satisfying my inner Planter, I ignored the warning signs, glorified his good qualities and downplayed the bad.
That's when I realized the parallels: Lessons are repeated until they are learned.

Through many conversations with my therapist, it became increasingly evident my desperate need to make a relationship work was directly tied to not knowing my self-worth. Once I graduated college and lost weight, people told me I was "a catch," but the 12-year-old fat girl inside me who had to fight for any morsel of positive attention from the opposite sex shouted louder.

Stopping a relationship felt a lot like giving up and proving Pre-Teen Toni right. It meant I'd have to go back out into the dating pool and expose myself to more potential rejection.

It also meant I'd have to live up to the standards of what people told me I could get. Family and friends would say, "You'll meet your match one day. He's out there somewhere." It left me dumbfounded. How did they know who my match was when I didn't even know it myself?

And that's when I identified the problem. I always knew I wanted to be in a relationship but never set standards of what that would look like. Similar to my weight-loss journey, I always knew weight loss was the goal, but I never clearly identified how I wanted to feel once I lost the weight or the person I wanted to become afterward.

Then, my therapist led me through a meditation technique to help center my thoughts and reflect on this pattern. We've done this type of grounding work before, but this time was different. Something finally clicked, and it was truly *groundbreaking* for me.

She had me close my eyes, slow down my thoughts, breathe deeply and pay attention to where my breath got stuck. "Breathe in through your nose, into your belly, then push the air out of your mouth," she instructed.

After about three breaths, she asked if I felt it strongest anywhere in my body. I *definitely* did.

It was in my throat. Like a lozenge was stuck in there. But it wasn't harming me. If anything, it helped me feel more *alive*.

I was nearly choking, but I was breathing. It was a euphoric feeling. Then, the blood rushed to my brain and the answer behind why I've never truly defined what I wanted in a partner, for my body, and most importantly, *myself*, became crystal clear: I was afraid of being let down. At that point, I had no more excuses. I had lost weight. I had a thriving career. I felt healthy. I was finally financially independent. I had a great group of friends. In short, I had my shit together. Everyone couldn't understand why I was single. And I agreed with them, deep down. But deeper down, the fear took over. In my gut, I knew why I was single. I had kept my dating expectations low because I didn't think I deserved someone better than that. But now, I was bringing great things to the table, which meant I had to up my standards. But by upping my standards, that meant a real potential for being let down, and letting others down.

The feeling in my throat symbolized my fear of speaking out and sharing what I really wanted *out loud* only added to the immense amount of pressure I already felt to achieve things. It was easier to play it safe and settle for mediocrity.

But the more time I spent sitting across from my therapist, defining my values and uncovering what was important to me, the harder it was for me to be OK with being *just* OK. The only way I was going to stop settling and start feeling significant was by acknowledging the younger parts of me that continued to interrupt my metamorphosis. To this day, I continue to whisper to the hurt, little girl inside of me that she has nothing to prove because she was worthy of being loved then, is worthy of being loved now and always will be.

Here's the parallel: As I began to dive into my relationship issues, it was impossible to ignore they were nearly identical to the issues I had with food.

My thought process was the same. My behavior was the same. My emotional swings were the same. The way they both took over my life was the same.

Just as I was prone to disappearing into any relationship I entered, I was equally likely to become engulfed in changing my diet. I was all-or-nothing in both aspects of my life.

In the "all-in" phases, my default setting was to diet *hard*, generally obsessed with food, categorizing "good" vs. "bad" and eating (or not eating) according to an ever-increasing number of restrictions to maintain a calorie deficit.

But during the "nothing" phases, my process was to turn my brain off. Being *on* was an exhausting experience. In desperate need of a break from the mental rigor of trying to determine if the ROI of a single bite of food was high enough to justify eating it, I simply stopped.

In those phases, I'd eat whatever happened to be in front of me, sometimes binging, sometimes not. This was as close to food freedom as I could imagine.

Most of the time, I was *on*,[7] my entire life arranged and rearranged to support my weight-loss efforts.

---

[7] Something worth discussing here is the outward expression of being "on." In these periods, during which I was eating what most people consider to be healthy foods, I was encouraged by my family and friends. In a vacuum, my exercise and nutrition habits weren't inherently bad. But in context, they were symptoms of a larger issue. Our culture socially rewards us not just for being thin but also for getting thin; we're applauded for losing weight and for the methods we use to get there.

In contrast, when we gain weight, we lose social capital. Within the range of norms, we're considered less attractive. Our lifestyle (continued on page 55)

I'll never forget that day in therapy when I realized trying to make exercise plans and sample menus from magazines fit into *one* part of my life was a direct reflection of how I was trying to force the men I dated to fit into my goals.

No matter how much evidence I had this just *wasn't working*, I kept finding ways to explain it away or hide it under a series of excuses just like a Planter would do.

I was so caught up in making it work long term it never occurred to me it wasn't even working in the short term.

Once I'd become aware of the parallels, I couldn't unsee them. They were everywhere.

RELATIONSHIP	FOOD
• He only gets angry with me when I ask too many questions • He doesn't get along with my family and friends so I can keep them separate • We used to be so happy and in love. It must be me. I just need to work harder • At least we're not *as bad* as ... (insert unhealthy relationship couple here)	• I only get *hangry* once a day • The stress of trying to stick to healthy options from a restaurant menu is too much, so I just won't go out with my friends • I used to be able to stick to this plan. It must be me. I just need to work harder • At least I can eat *some* carbs

From that moment on, I was determined to break from the ever-repeating cycle in both areas of my life.

Over the next several months, I worked through my issues with food and with relationships, first untangling them from one another and then analyzing them separately.

As fate would have it, just as I was going through this process, my dietitian practice began to experience some real growth. Before I knew it, I was working with 20 new clients and almost all of them had an experience similar to my own.

I couldn't help but think thousands of others I didn't know and wasn't working with yet would also benefit from learning how and why we diet how we date.

♥ ♥ ♥

WHAT WE GET WRONG

Society fosters the belief that if we're not actively trying to take care of our bodies, we're doing something wrong. Similarly, if we're not in a relationship, we must have some fatal flaws.

This shows up consistently across most of Western culture: The generalized obsession with the pursuit, often with the goal of some quantifiable measure of progress.

We're encouraged to be consistently exerting effort to modify our bodies through fitness, chasing the imaginary ideal of whatever we consider to be an acceptable size. When it comes to progress, we're under constant pressure to seek out, enter, dive into and advance romance, the goal being the rapid ascension of the relationship escalator, lifting us toward wedded bliss.

We use both dieting and dating to make us feel good. Yet, once the novelty fades, we lose sight of why we started in the first place. We begin to settle for something less ideal

---

choices are questioned and judged as unhealthy. We're shamed for everything from the food we eat to the clothes we wear. We're reminded, often not subtly, that we can lose weight with a little effort and that doing so should be our preference.

Being validated for one set of behaviors and shamed for the opposite instills an innate understanding that only one is "acceptable." The cycle this generates takes most of us years to recognize and many more to address and disrupt.

or spend endless amounts of energy trying to replicate the honeymoon phase. We confuse sacrifice with compromise, ignore the gut feelings and wait it out until we finally find a reason to stay. Here's that Planter showing up again.

With this pressure, we often get caught up in the first few things that present themselves, try them for a while and then get upset when they don't work out. But if you paid attention to the red flags, you'd know they were never there in the first place.

The most common culprit we fall for are fad diets.

HOW TO SPOT A FAD DIET

THERE ISN'T A SET APPROACH TO SPOTTING A FAD DIET, BUT THESE GENERAL TIPS CAN HELP. FAD DIETS TEND TO HAVE:

- Recommendations that promise a quick fix.
- Claims that sound too good to be true.
- Simplistic conclusions drawn from a complex study.
- Recommendations based on a single study.
- Dramatic statements that are refuted by reputable scientific organizations.
- Lists of "good" and "bad" foods.
- Recommendations made to help sell a book or product.
- Recommendations based on studies published without peer review.
- Recommendations from studies that ignore differences among individuals or groups.
- Elimination of one or more of the five food groups (fruits, vegetables, grains, protein foods, and dairy) or subgroups (grains, dairy, fruit).

RESOURCE: https://my.clevelandclinic.org/health/articles/9476-fad-diets

The word, "fad" says it all because it insinuates something is temporary, yet we hope the results last forever. But the truth is, if you like the results you're getting, you'll have to keep putting in that effort to continue to get that in return.

CHAPTER 5

SCALES DON'T MEASURE
WHAT MATTERS

"Imagine what women would be able to do
with all the time wasted thinking about how to
lose the last 5 pounds."

- *Dr. Aviva Romm,* holistic medicine practitioner

I hope by now, you understand your body size does not determine your worth. But what about your health?

As a child, I fell into the 95th percentile for my height and weight. Even as an adult when I shifted my eating habits to healthier choices, increased my physical activity to above the daily recommendation and lost inches, I still had a Body Mass Index (BMI) that categorized me as "overweight."[8]

Being told by doctors to "watch my weight" to prevent falling into the "obese" category was not new to me. And the more I heard it, the more frustrated I'd become.

My doctor never asked me about my diet or how active I was. All of that was assumed because of two numbers: My height and weight.

Want to know if you're healthy or not? Take your weight in kilograms, divide it by the square of your height in meters,

---

[8] More on BMI later on in this chapter.

and *voila*, you're either doomed to develop a myriad of chronic diseases or you have nothing to worry about.

Without knowing one's sex, activity level, eating habits or medical history, someone who weighs at least 30 pounds over the "standard" is determined to be unhealthy and is encouraged, scratch that, *pushed* to "watch their weight," as if they didn't already live in a society pressuring them to do that.

And those who fit into the "normal" category are exempt from the shame and are told everything "looks" good, regardless if this person lives a sedentary lifestyle and the only vegetable they eat is ketchup on their french fries.

Despite all my weight-loss efforts, I was still being told to try harder. I wasn't even "obese," but I was not-so-subtly being instructed to change myself. This made me wonder how those in the "obese" cateogry felt. I learned to put these categories in quotes after reading the book *Anti-Diet* by Registered Dietitian Christy Harrison. In it, she explains, in a polite way, that "We don't have an obesity epidemic. We have a weight stigma epidemic."

There are much more efficient ways to check for body fat percentage and body composition[9] than using BMI, but apparently, the $72+ billion wrapped up in the diet industry is better spent trapping you in a vicious cycle rather than giving you more accurate forms of measurements like skinfold thickness measurements (with calipers), underwater

---

[9] Body composition is a term used to describe the difference between your Fat Free Mass, or FFM from your Fat Mass (FM). Fat Free Mass is everything from your muscle to your bones, blood, and organs. Your Fat Mass is the adipose tissue stored in your body, in the form of subcutaneous fat, which is what we see in the mirror, and visceral fat, which is between the organs. Discussions of body composition usually center around your body fat percentage, or the total percentage of your weight composed of adipose tissue. This is generally considered to be a more accurate measure of health than the BMI; but, like the BMI is imperfect. The ranges of what's considered normal, healthy, or ideal are based on imperfect formulas, and, in my view, give us another number to be worried about. Scale weight, body composition and the BMI are all decent tools--until the exact moment we start using them as the only measure of success.

weighing, bioelectrical impedance, dual-energy X-ray absorptiometry (DXA) or isotope dilution. However, these methods are either expensive or need to be conducted by highly trained personnel. Therefore, they're often not used, and, even if they were, they still don't tell the *whole* story.

One of the more recent analyses of obesity by Harvard School of Public Health[10] showed two-thirds (69%) of adults ages 20 or older are categorized as overweight or obese based on BMI.

The study goes on to show there are moderate correlations between obesity and chronic diseases. But if I learned anything between obtaining a Bachelors of Science and Masters in Nutrition, correlation does *not* imply causation. Even if it did, I'd still question the accuracy of this statistic because the results measuring "at risk" are based on the BMI calculator, which we've already established as a BS computation.

Here's the part that's ludacris. Despite knowing all of this, I still hated that Fit Toni, a Registered Dietitian, someone who helped people lose weight, fell into the overweight category. This bothered me when I was young, and it upset me more and more as I got older. The harder I tried, the more disappointing that, after all the work and effort I put in, it still wasn't "good enough."

WHEN 5 POUNDS ISN'T JUST 5 POUNDS, AND 'NORMAL' ISN'T NORMAL

It didn't matter how active I was, how healthy I ate or even if I lost some weight, I *still* fell in the "overweight" category. My highest BMI of 29 (right on the cusp of obesity) went down

---

[10] https://www.hsph.harvard.edu/obesity-prevention-source/obesity-trends/obesity-rates-worldwide/

to 25 when I lost 25 pounds, which was a full 13.5% of my original weight. I knew this was good for me because what the BMI chart doesn't tell you is that even a modest weight loss (5 to 10% of your total body weight) is likely to produce health benefits, such as improvements in blood pressure and cholesterol.

So even though I was still in the "overweight" category, I knew I was healthier, especially because I got there with a nutrition and exercise plan that felt good to me. I enjoyed the process. It was part of my lifestyle.

Despite the 25-pound weight loss, I didn't fit the criteria to be considered "normal" by BMI standards. But if I could lose another five pounds, I would.

I already had a great foundation. I ate protein at every meal, almost always including fruit or vegetables, paired my snacks with healthy fats and listened to my hunger cues. I already lost 25 pounds, so what's five more?

What I didn't know then but later learned was five more pounds was not just five more pounds. Five more pounds was the difference between food *freedom* and *obsession*. To lose those five pounds and keep it off, I had to count every macronutrient and stay in a deficit of 1,000 calories a day, increase my strength-training program from four days a week to five and commit to cardio four days a week. Because the calorie count was too low, I chose to try Intermittent Fasting as a way to prevent the temptation to go over. So I'd often go to bed hungry, sometimes not eating or drinking after 4 p.m. because I knew anything in my stomach (even water) would make the scale go up.

I always backslid to my younger days when I got so caught

up in needing a certain outcome, I stopped seeing the warnings telling me to slow down and reassess. It started getting harder. My anxiety about food was coming back, and I forgot about my own quote: "If you don't fall in love with the process, you'll be forever disappointed with the progress."

It took a couple months, but I did it. I finally got into the "normal" category, weighing in at 155. That number was a place I thought I'd be OK to stop at and just maintain, but I wanted to see how much more I could lose. I thought to myself: "145 would look perfect."

My mind was motivated, but then my body started breaking down.

SAVED BY SICKNESS

Between the extreme caloric restriction, the frequent workouts without adequate recovery and the intense mental exertion it took to keep it all going, things reached a predictable breaking point.

First came the onset of extreme fatigue. Any amount of exertion beyond walking caused dizziness, so my exercise habits needed to change. My doctor instructed me to stop working out entirely, but I didn't listen. Instead, I gradually reduced them, fighting it every step of the way as my high-intensity training dwindled to nothing and my half-hearted cardio sessions came to a halt.

My body was a bit of a disaster. My cortisol levels, which is a hormone secreted during times of stress, was all over the place, which accounted for my fatigue. Later, I was diagnosed with Epstein-Barr virus, resulting in muscle aches and weakness. Finally, I also developed SIBO (small intestinal bacterial overgrowth), which manifested itself with extreme bloating and intestinal discomfort whenever I ate anything.

I felt like one gigantic mess. Whether it was caused by the stress I put on myself or the illnesses, it didn't matter.

The answer to healing was to rest and remove the calorie deficit, feeding and nourishing my body instead of waging war on it. In retrospect, I see how clearly every red flag was being waved at me to stop going down the destructive path of disordered eating and body dysmorphia.

It took an illness to stop me and, at the time, I was disappointed and frustrated, but it's easy to see now that getting sick was the best thing that could've happened to me. If I hadn't gotten sick, my disordered eating would have most likely developed into a full-blown eating disorder, and you'd be reading a very different book.

Seeing the lengths it took me to get to a "normal" weight, I know now that's not normal for me and certainly not *my* healthiest weight, which meant I needed to define what my healthiest weight was.

When I sat and reflected on this, I realized it wasn't a number at all. But that's not what most doctors tell you.

USING THE RIGHT METRICS FOR SUCCESS

I used to think being healthy meant giving up all of my favorite foods, working out whether I felt like it or not and putting in *maximum* amounts of effort *no matter what.* I was so fixated on losing 20 pounds, I was ignoring my body asking me to re-direct my path. I didn't realize the immense amount of pressure I put on myself was doing more harm than good.

But after many fights with the scale, I see what matters most: *My sanity.*

I'm still committed to being the healthiest version of me, but, this time, it's with a better definition of what that means.

My physical health matters, but if I find myself obsessing over the size of an avocado, beating myself up for "only" working out for 20 minutes, or feeling more down than proud overall, then I know it's time to reassess the goal.

If you want to lose the weight and keep it off, then you're going to have to get used to non-drastic, slow changes.

Every week won't be a progress week.

If you're striving for sustainable results in your weight-loss journey, you'll have to get used to not seeing the number on the scale go down weekly.

You'll have to accept the fact that the old way of crash dieting, although tempting, will only lead you back to where you were six months ago.

You'll need to trust the process and start using other forms of measurement to motivate you to keep going.

Regardless of the machines, equations or methods used to measure our weight, we need to switch the mission to achieve *body goals* versus *self-care goals*. Eat well because it makes you more energetic, exercise to improve your mood, meditate to reduce stress, get a good night's sleep, and *then* see where your weight falls.

OBJECTIVE VS. SUBJECTIVE MEASUREMENTS

Sane and sustainable weight loss go hand-in-hand. For something to be sustainable, it needs to be sane, and, trust me, if you do something extreme or unsustainable for a long enough time, you won't be logical.

To keep things balanced, it's important to look at what you're measuring and why because how you relate to the issue *is* the issue.

If you could have endless amounts of energy, wear your clothes with confidence and know you were doing your best to prevent or treat disease, would you still obsess over the number on the scale? The size of your pants? Your reflection in the mirror? Or how your stomach looks when you're sitting?

One of the most significant issues affecting both our approach to health and our self-esteem is the way we're taught to attach meaning to measurements.

Whether it's scale weight, BMI or body composition, we're given a set of numbers to aim toward, as if the entirety of our body and experience of health can be broken down to neat, numerical representations.

Once we choose which of these magical numbers is the one we should use to define ourselves, we get more numbers: Calories, waist circumference or grams of protein.

There's nothing wrong with numbers and measurements. Used correctly, they're helpful. And, truthfully, they're easy to measure and, to some degree, easy to manage. We see when they go up or down, which may give us some insight into what behaviors to alter in order to accomplish our goals.

Again, these metrics are helpful *if used properly and carefully.* All of these numbers are what we call objective criteria.

Objective criteria are things which can be quantified: Pounds, calories, macronutrients, body size and circumference. Then, there are more of the advanced systems used to rate things like body fat percentage.

What they don't account for is the subjective criteria.

Subjective criteria are all about how you feel, which makes things more nebulous. Things like self-esteem, energy levels, general happiness, body image and, in particular, how you feel about the objective criteria are unquantifiable and, therefore, harder to define.

If your goal is to improve your body image, weight loss can be a part of that. But, if you focus is on weight loss alone, you're always going to want to keep moving the goalpost. When you finally diet down to a size 8, you'll start to ask yourself "What would happen if I fit into a size 4?" Somehow, it'll never feel like it's enough, and your body image will still suffer.

The key is to set subjective goals and use your pursuit of objective goals to support that. The process of learning about what your body needs and how to take care of it can teach you about yourself in a way that focusing on weight loss alone can't.

Working toward a subjective experience of improving your body image can help you lose weight, but the entry point is different.

In contrast, zoning in on weight loss exclusively often leads to ignoring your body's resistance to the approach you're taking.

Working towards objective goals to accomplish subjective goals doesn't work. There are apps and devices to help you measure your sleep, and while it's helpful to know how many hours and minutes you slept, that doesn't really tell you how rested you feel or how much energy you will have the next morning.

The truth is *you can't diet your way to happiness*. Losing weight to fit into a new dress may make you feel better about the way you look at the moment, but learning to love the way you look will make you happy no matter your dress size.

On the other hand, concentrating on the subjective--how you feel about what's happening during the process--will help you to establish a healthier relationship with your nutritional habits. And it'll help you stick to them, leading to the objective goals you had originally set.

The real magic behind going about it in this way is you'll feel happier during the entire process. Because changing how you feel about whether or not you "need" to lose 10 pounds is going to have a *much* greater impact on your life than losing the 10 pounds.

SUBJECTIVE EXPERIENCE MATTERS MORE

Let's play out this scenario: You've been eating healthy, exercising, prioritizing sleep, doing "all-the-things," and you feel really proud of yourself.

You've been putting in the work for a week or so and want to see if your efforts have paid off, so you excitedly step on the scale, expecting a drop.

But it doesn't drop. Not even a little bit. It's exactly the same. Or worse, it goes up!

Your immediate reaction is to get upset, followed by frustration and thoughts of "what's the point?" echo in your head.

But then you remember what you learned earlier: There are different ways to track your progress, and the scale isn't always the most reliable one.

Plus, you're not doing this for a number. You're doing this for a feeling. Don't let a machine dictate how you feel.

The lesson here is twofold. First, it's important to know what you're doing *is* working, despite what you just saw. Trust the process because slow change is real change. Second, you need to find some subjective victories to measure things beyond the numbers.

YOUR RELATIONSHIP WITH FOOD

We live in a society in which disordered eating has been normalized.

Cutting out whole food groups, intentionally skipping meals and following strict nutrition plans is the trendy thing to do. And it's what most people do to "fix" their eating habits, but those are the exact reasons why their eating habits need fixing in the first place.

Disordered eating is used to describe a range of irregular

eating behaviors that include some of the following:

- Frequent dieting
- Chronic weight fluctuations
- Rigid routines surrounding food
- Feelings of guilt associated with eating
- Preoccupation with food, weight and body image that negatively impact quality of life
- Feelings of loss of control around food
- Using exercise, food restriction, fasting or purging to "make up for bad foods" consumed
- Disconnect between hunger and fullness feelings

Whether you struggle with an eating disorder or disordered eating, both are serious conditions that need to be addressed by a nutrition professional.

You need individualized attention, ongoing support and a realistic plan to unlearn these unhealthy habits and create a clear path toward building healthier ones. Here are some telltale signs your relationship with food is healing:

- You no longer think about it *constantly* (before, during, after, between and even in your dreams)
- Decreased anxiety around food
- Greater ease ordering what you really want on the menu versus what you "should" (a.k.a. the "healthiest" thing listed)
- You implement other ways to cope with emotions so food is no longer your only outlet
- You no longer classify certain foods as "off-limits," "good," or "bad," therefore you binge less often and no longer feel the need to hide eating certain foods
- Experience little guilt, shame or regret after eating
- You stop skipping meals intentionally to "save your

calories" or cease exercising excessively to "make room for food"
- You eat when you're hungry and stop when you're full more often than not
- If you do overeat, you accept it and move on rather than feeling the need to punish yourself or make up for it by restricting yourself afterward

BOWEL MOVEMENTS

We all poop, and if you have a healthy digestive system, you should be going at least once per day. Nonetheless, it wasn't until I started working as a RD I learned most people don't and when they do, it takes much longer than it should. Constipation, diarrhea, constantly feeling bloated or a combo of all of the above is more common than you think, but it doesn't have to be that way.

Having to run to find the nearest restroom in the middle of a conversation at the most inconvenient of places or missing out on events because you're stuck in the bathroom does *not* have to be your norm.

The "3-3-3" rule is a good guide to know if your bowel movements are regular. You should go no more than three times a day, no less than once every three days, and when you "do the doo," it should take no more than three minutes.

Often small changes like drinking more water, consuming more fiber, incorporating foods rich in pre- and probiotics, managing stress and engaging in movement are usually enough to help regulate your bowels.

It's probably not the cleanest lesson I've ever taught but definitely the most necessary one. Because, let's be honest, walking around with a full belly of waste for days on end is not comfortable.

HAIR, NAILS AND SKIN

For every weight-loss article in any female-targeted magazine, there are at least two more about how to cover up acne, style your hair or what color to paint your nails.
What one eats or drinks can significantly impact the glow of a person's skin, thicken their hair and even strengthen their nails. Yes, some people are more acne-prone than others, just like some people are more constipation-prone than others, but regardless, similar to improving your gut health, small changes in your diet can rejuvenate one's hair, skin and nails.

Dairy, chocolate, sugar and fried foods get a bad reputation for causing acne, but that's only when consumed in excess without increasing your water[11] and protein consumption.[12]

Your skin is the largest organ in the body and serves as a visible gauge for how changing your habits can improve your health.

ENERGY LEVELS

Maybe it's because you're sleeping deeper, eating better, managing your stress and moving your body, but whatever it is, you're more energetic. You're hitting new personal records in the gym. You no longer feel too tired to play with your

---

[11] Although everyone's nutritional needs are uniquely based on a variety of factors like age, gender, body composition, medical history and activity level, here's a general rule of thumb to know if you're drinking enough water: Total body weight (pounds) divided by 2 = total fluid ounces of water needed each day. For example, someone who weighs 150 pounds needs 75 fluid ounces of water per day. That equals more than nine cups of water daily.

[12] There are many equations to help estimate protein needs based on body weight, gender and physical activity, but I find my clients are most successful when they start with a goal of incorporating 20 to 30 grams of protein at each meal and at least one snack with at least 10 grams of protein.

kids. You have the energy to go out after work, and you're able to accomplish your daily tasks with ease. You're no longer fighting to keep your head upright.

But if you rely heavily on caffeine and find yourself always needing that second cup, you may be putting a Band-Aid on the wound. If, without that second cup, you feel tired no matter how much sleep you get, you're moody, angry and short-tempered and what used to excite you is now a complete drag, it's time to assess if the effort you're putting in is worth the return on investment.

BODY IMAGE

If you want to change the size of your body, that's okay. Just don't hate it along the way. Loving your body is a result of taking care of it.

Rather than trying to achieve body positivity every day, practice body acceptance. Body acceptance means when you look in the mirror and don't love what you see, don't get defeated, take a step back and remind yourself that it's OK.

Some days, you'll like your reflection, and some days you won't. That's normal.[13]

No matter how you feel, accept your body as *yours*—a body that deserves to be respected by you, and everyone else, *no matter what.*

---

[13] Here are five things you can do when having a bad body image day: 1. Acknowledge it as a moment 2. Ask yourself, "What's actually bothering me?" 3. Focus on gratitude, what can your body do for you? 4. Take a break from social media 5. Replace criticism with compassion, remind yourself of the amazing person that you are!

How to know your body image is improving:

- You're less worried about what other people think of you
- You spend less time getting dressed in the morning
- You enjoy going shopping for new clothes
- You wear outfits you used to say "only a skinny person can wear"

MENTAL HEALTH

When people think of getting healthy, they often think of diet and exercise, but your health is so much more than that. As discussed earlier, improving your diet and exercise regimen can enhance your physical health, which often positively affects your mental health. However, when taken to the extreme, it can do the opposite.

Life is to be enjoyed, so if your diet includes foods you don't like and engaging in physical activity you hate, then you need to re-assess what you're doing and why.

In the process, make sure you're not neglecting other key areas to your wellness like self care[14], stress management[15] and forming healthy relationships[16].

---

[14] Commit to at least one activity per week that makes you feel like you're taking care of yourself, for instance get a facial, a manicure or take a bubble bath.

[15] Try going to bed and waking up at the same time daily. If your schedule doesn't allow it, create a nighttime routine that includes a winding down period of no phone use, so your body knows when it's time to go to sleep. Allow for quiet time so you can process your thoughts. Stop saying yes to commitments you don't want to do. Learn to be OK with doing less.

[16] Surround yourself with people who love and believe in you. Set boundaries with those who take, complain and put you or others down.

WHAT YOU MEASURE MATTERS

Numbers and measurements can be helpful, but they rarely tell the whole story. If they're stressing you out more than they're helping you out, then it's time to re-assess the emphasis you're putting on them.

The scale doesn't know you had a rough week and, despite your history of stress eating, you managed to resist reacting to the emotions.

The laminated, 1990s-era BMI chart hanging in your doctor's office doesn't know you're sleeping better, have more energy and, as a result, are more present with your family and friends.

When you care solely about the objective measurements, you'll be disappointed more often than not. Instead, take the action steps required to improve your overall health and make your subjective experience the center of attention.

Do that consistently, day-in and day-out, and I assure you'll eventually see the results you crave, but, more importantly, you'll be proud of yourself.

CHAPTER 6

DEFINING WHAT
MATTERS TO YOU

"All she wanted was the effort that she gave."

- R.H. Sin, Self love poet

Everyone dreams of a partner who's attractive, charming, funny, educated, well-mannered and successful. You know, the kind of person who's close (but not too close) to their family and has a group of friends they can hang with while you spend time with yours.

Those attributes are appealing, especially when they come together in a single package, but people aren't packages. And traits people have are more than boxes you want to check off your wish list.

We need to think not only of these traits individually, but how the person is using them collectively.

For example, the number one most desirable trait listed in countless surveys is "a sense of humor." And that's great. But what does that really mean? Do you want someone who's able to laugh at a joke or someone who is funny? And what kind of funny are you looking for? Are they witty and sarcastic, or do they love to goof around?

Most importantly, when you begin looking at the importance

of certain traits measured against the rest, how much does a "high score" in one area override a lower score in another?

Just *how* good does a person's sense of humor need to be in order to outweigh the fact they struggle financially? And while a sense of humor tops the list when we fill out surveys, in truth, we all know people who often go for sexy over funny or successful and ambitious over kind and compassionate.

Nothing about this is innately wrong, of course. Everyone has the right to decide what matters most to them when searching for a partner.

Whether it's subconscious or not, some part of us is doing complex emotional calculus, processing equations like: *"If they have a great job but take life too seriously, is that enough to hold onto?"*

Instead, we need to analyze what we *think* matters and define what *actually* matters. Just as there's no perfect person who will score a 10-out-of-10 in every category, there's no premade diet that's going to immediately get you to all of your nutritional goals while fitting perfectly into your lifestyle.

If you take a look at the chart below, you'll see how big of an attitude adjustment we need to make to find what will help us succeed in the long run.

WHAT WE THINK MATTERS	WHAT ACTUALLY MATTERS
• Fast weight loss	• Slow weight loss
• Amount of weight lost	• Amount of weight maintained
• BMI	• Body composition
• Clothing Size	• How our clothes fit
• The opinion of others	• The opinion of ourselves
• Physical Health	• Physical and Mental Health
• Going "All In" (perfection)	• Committed but flexible (progress)
• Body goals	• Self-care

You've got to assess how important each of your goals is, in what order you're going to prioritize them, what you're willing to do to achieve that and over what length of time.

We want to look a certain way, but most aesthetic goals require compromise. It's up to us to decide if the juice is worth the squeeze.

In the previous chapter, we established the things we need to measure outside of the numbers that appear on the scale. We discussed things that mattered on a subjective level. Now, it's time to measure them.

I've outlined a process to rate your current experience of everything from your digestion to your energy levels. This is the same exercise I go through with my clients on our weekly check-ins to create a customized plan.

On a scale of 1-5, you're going to rank where you currently are.

1	2	3	4	5
DIGESTION				
Constipation/ Diarrhea Weekly		Bloating and gas often		Have a solid & smooth BM 1-2/day
PERSONAL RECORDS (PRS IN THE GYM / TRACK / HOME WORKOUT)				
Workouts feel harder without changing routine				Able to increase weights or decrease mileage time
ENERGY LEVELS				
Can't keep your head up				Energizer bunny!
WELL-BEING / MOOD / MENTAL HEALTH				
Cranky, Angry, Sad				Upbeat, positive, content
HAIR / SKIN / NAILS				
Hair falling out, nails breaking, skin broken out				Strong hair and nails, clear skin
BODY IMAGE / SELF CONFIDENCE				
No matter what you wear "nothing looks good"				Grateful for what your body can do for you
YOUR RELATIONSHIP WITH FOOD				
Can't be around food without feeling anxious				Eat based off your wants and needs, without guilt

Now, go back and note where you'd like to be in each category. After that, decide how you'd like to prioritize them and why.

I've encouraged you to go through this exercise for a few reasons:

- If you don't identify what's important to you, you'll be chasing all the things at once and will lose your focus
- Self awareness and introspection is everything. You have to bring them both in order to know where to go next
- Using the number scale over time shows you where you are and how far you've come

Now that you understand why this is a crucial step, stop reading. Go grab a pen (or make some mental notes) and identify what's important to you to avoid being forever disappointed with your results.

THE SCIENCE OF WEIGHT LOSS

Losing weight isn't rocket science, but it *is* science. Understanding how the body's machinery works is an essential part of making the correct decisions and taking actions that align with your goals.

In the end, you don't need a degree in nutritional science or an Olympic coach's understanding of biomechanics. Still, a baseline understanding of a few metabolic processes is the surest way to avoid unhealthy habits or falling prey to things that don't work.

Below, I'm going to break down the basics.

CALORIES IN VS. CALORIES OUT (CICO)

At the core of every diet is the law of thermodynamics. When applied to the human metabolism, food is converted to energy, which is then used by the body to perform activities.

It's an equation of energy balance. If you consume more

calories than the total daily energy expenditure (TDEE), you'll gain weight. If you take in as much as you burn, you'll maintain weight. If you consume less than you expend (also known as a calorie deficit), you'll lose weight.

That's why, regardless of the plan a person follows like Atkins, keto, South Beach, Jenny Craig, etc., as long as they stay in a calorie deficit, it will be "effective" for weight loss.

In 2010, Mark Haub, a professor of human nutrition at Kansas State University, ate a Twinkie every three hours, instead of meals, limiting himself to fewer than 1,800 calories a day, without changing his energy expenditure.

Before dieting, Haubs' TDEE was around 2,600, putting him in a negative energy balance of 800 calories per day. At the end of the 10-week experiment, he lost 27 pounds.[17]

He's not the only one. In 2019, fitness writer and podcaster Jordan Syatt conducted a similar experiment, eating a Big Mac for 30 days.[18] Syatt's experiment, which he dubbed the "Big Mac Challenge" (or BMC), was partially inspired by the 2004 documentary *Super Size Me* in which filmmaker Morgan Spurlock ate McDonald's every day for a month to demonstrate the dangers of fast-food overconsumption, which he considers to be a fixture of the American diet.

The difference between *Super Size Me* and Syatt's BMC was the attention paid to overall energy intake. While Spurlock intentionally ate too much, Syatt maintained a caloric deficit, consuming roughly 1,500 calories per day, 540 of those precious calories came from the iconic Big Mac.

---

[17] I'm not condoning doing this yourself, of course, but am simply using it as an example.
[18] Also not suggesting you do this.

During Syatt's 30-day experiment, he dropped 7 pounds, demonstrating even when the food quality isn't ideal, energy balance is still the primary determinant for weight loss.

While two self-conducted studies, each with one participant, don't show direct cause and effect, these are great examples of the hundreds of more extensive studies conducted about calories-in-calories-out (CICO) over the past century.

Here's the kicker. Even though it "worked," it didn't include measures for non-scale markers like bowel movements, hunger and energy levels. If they were included, you'd most likely find out their bowel movements were irregular, their appetite was high and their energy was running low.

If weight loss is a goal for you, the CICO equation needs to be involved in your diet planning. However, it shouldn't stop there. You must also consider the macronutrient composition of your diet and the quality of food for optimal progress and, more importantly, sustainability.

In theory, this sounds so simple, but basic physics isn't so basic when we throw being human into the mix. Cravings, juggling a busy schedule and living in a technologically advanced lifestyle where you don't even need to leave your bed to turn on the lights makes it difficult to achieve a calorie deficit.

Mainly, as people lose weight, the body, in its attempt to retain fat, becomes more energy-efficient and reduces its basal metabolic rate (BMR). The body becomes resistant to weight loss in an effort to conserve energy, thus requiring fewer and fewer calories to achieve weight loss and even maintain weight.

Initially, following a low-calorie plan is easy, but sustainable weight loss does not happen overnight. You need to put in consistent effort if you like the results it gives you in return. Let's play out this scenario:

You've made the decision to start tracking your calories again, but this time, you've set your calorie goal lower than before. You have the motivation and finally feel like you have control over your food choices. You even lose a little weight. At first.

But what happens when you've expended your energy on both ends? Eventually, the restriction leads to low energy, lack of enjoyment of food and hunger kicks in.

Suddenly, your control starts to slip. At this point, you're so ravenous, it doesn't matter how focused and motivated you are. Your physical cues lead to an eating frenzy. You feel defeated.

The resultant binge isn't a lack of willpower, it's your body's way of fighting back against the caloric deficit. But without the knowledge of how the body functions, you blame yourself. The frustration for overeating brings you right back to trying what "worked" before, except it's not working. If it was, would you have to keep starting over and over again?

The worst part of this cycle is the more you stay in it, the more challenging weight loss becomes. Your metabolism adapts, making each new attempt of weight loss more complicated than the previous one.

Regardless of the amount of weight loss programs you've tried, let this message be the reason you choose to end the restriction and embrace balance instead.

If you caught on to anything I've shared thus far, you know your health is more than the number on the scale.

Health is not just about what you take away but what you add.

QUALITY OF FOOD

It's a lot easier to achieve a caloric deficit without feeling deprived when you work on adding more nutrient-dense foods.

Shift your focus away from eating less and, instead, to adding *more* things like these:

- Soup: Studies show consuming soup before a meal can significantly reduce total meal calorie intake up to 20% compared to having no soup. Best choices include clear broth and veggies, chunky vegetable soup or puréed vegetable soup
- Salad: Similar studies show eating a salad before meals reduces calorie intake by 7-12%. Note, this is only effective if the salad is low in calories and nutrient-dense. Meaning, just lettuce with lots of dressing and cheese doesn't count. Keep it basic: Lettuce, tomatoes, cucumbers and carrots with 1-2 tablespoons of dressing
- Soluble fiber: In general, fiber can help you feel full, but soluble fiber holds more water and increases bulk in your digestive tract, making it feel even more filling. Foods like oatmeal, oat bran, barley, chia/flax seeds, beans, squash, potatoes, pears, apples, citrus fruits and strawberries are great examples

HORMONAL ADAPTATIONS

Our bodies are designed to protect us. Even though we live in an era where food is readily available, our bodies haven't caught on to that yet.

As a result of not getting what it needs, whether through macronutrient restriction like low-carb diets or extreme calorie restriction such as 1200kcal or less per day, your endocrine system begins secreting hormones to try to get us to eat.

Leptin (a hormone made by fat cells to decrease appetite) goes down, and ghrelin (a hormone that increases appetite) goes up, which is what signals hunger to the brain.

Neural factors such as dopamine also signal an increased desire for fatty foods after weight loss.

All of this encourages weight gain after diet-induced weight loss and continues for at least one year after weight reduction. This is a vicious cycle: Increased hunger and decreased satiety, leading to overeating and increased subcutaneous body fat[19], which is the principal reason sustainable weight loss is so challenging.

So what can you do to minimize the aftermath besides removing the extreme calorie deficit?

---

[19] Subcutaneous fat is the fat stored just beneath your skin. Pinch your skin with your thumb and forefinger and you will be pinching subcutaneous fat. Visceral fat is the fat stored around your internal organs on the inside of your muscle wall. Subcutaneous fat is an important part of your body, but if your body is storing too much of it, you may be at a higher risk for health problems.

INCORPORATE ANTI-INFLAMMATORY FOODS

To explain this in scientific terms, leptin resistance is caused by fat cells, which produce large numbers of inflammatory chemicals or cytokines, blocking leptin's effects. Therefore, eating a healthful diet rich in anti-inflammatory foods, like antioxidants and Omega-3 fats, can improve leptin resistance. Examples include salmon, walnuts, chia seeds, avocado and olive oil.

IMPROVE YOUR SLEEP HYGIENE

Sleep deprivation studies show inadequate sleep (getting fewer than seven to nine hours per night) can increase ghrelin (your hunger hormone), enhancing your appetite and increasing cravings for sugary foods. Many studies have found sleep restriction leads to increased caloric consumption.

INCLUDE ALL FOOD GROUPS

Each food group represents a different set of macronutrients (carbohydrates, protein and fat), which the body needs to consume in large amounts daily to function optimally. Without eating carbohydrates, protein transport to the muscle becomes compromised. Inefficient fat intake decreases the absorption of essential nutrients. Inadequate protein intake contributes to blood sugar instability. Eat quality sources from each food group as often as you can. Here are some easy choices to make:

- Fruits in their whole form more than fruit juice
- Vegetables raw/slightly cooked more than turned to mush
- Proteins grilled, baked, broiled or steamed more often than fried

- Grains with greater than 3g of fiber per serving more than refined grains
- Fats that are liquid at room temperature more than solid
- Low fat dairy more than full fat

In short, each food group's macronutrients depend on each other: Without one macronutrient, the other can't do its job, which is why we need to eat them daily.

Then, focus on portion control to limit calorie intake.

RECOVERY FROM EXERCISE

Most people use exercise to achieve a more significant calorie deficit, forgetting that, without proper fueling, the body experiences more muscle soreness and fatigue. This makes training less than desirable and hitting personal records (PRs) much harder.

People often look to supplements to help with this. Although some research supports supplementing specific nutrients for active individuals, there won't be any significant changes without addressing food first.

Healthy eating and exercise go together like peanut butter and jelly. Good nutrition acts as a fuel source before and after a workout. And the harder you train, the more calories you'll need, specifically foods rich in carbohydrates (carbs).

Without consuming enough carbs, glycogen stores (which are the carbs in the muscles) drop significantly. And while some people may argue they're able to function with lower carbohydrate levels, there's a difference between "functioning" and performing optimally.

This is why ingestion of protein is also essential. Consuming 20 to 40 grams of protein post-workout will stimulate protein muscle synthesis (the build and repair muscle), and consuming adequate amounts of protein throughout the day will preserve muscle mass. Adequate protein intake helps keep the metabolism happy, rather than dropping too low.

In addition to carbs and protein, the body needs to ingest healthy fats. During exercise, oxidative stress occurs. While low levels of activity are necessary for muscles to adapt to exercise, strenuous exercise can lead to chronic inflammation, stressing the body's antioxidant systems. As previously established, consuming foods rich in Omega-3 fatty acids (antioxidants) will help counter this.

Last but certainly not least is water. Drinking enough water throughout the day will keep you properly hydrated, which is key to improving cognition, mood and even sleep quality, which is a vital process in recovering from workouts.

As exercise increases, fluids should contain sodium, particularly for those who sweat. Urine color should be light like lemonade, and there should be a plentiful amount.
Whether you identify as an active person or not, the root of fatigue, headaches, dry skin and stiff joints is often dehydration, so drink up.

HOW APPETITE AND SATIETY AFFECTS YOUR MOOD AND WELL BEING

What you eat dictates how you feel and how you feel dictates what you do.

Most people certainly want weight loss, but the *why* behind that desire is the real reason: To feel energized, confident and happy. And the *why* behind that takes it a level deeper. Most people believe more energy, confidence and an upbeat attitude will help them achieve what they truly desire, whether that means a more intimate connection with their partner, the guts to ask for a promotion, energy to play with their kids or finally putting their needs before everyone else's.

That's a tall order. It's hard to believe something as simple as modifying your nutrition can solve all this.

But I've seen it done, both personally and professionally. The more we practice self-care by making time to eat nutrient-dense foods, the more energy we have and the less irritable we are. The less irritated we are, the more we get along with our loved ones.

Think about times you've gone hours without eating when hunger turns to anger, commonly known as being "hangry." If you thought you're the only one who gets hangry and blows up at their partner when trying to choose which restaurant to go to for date night, you're not. There is a real medical explanation behind this: A biochemical reaction due to low blood sugar.

When you haven't eaten for a while, your blood glucose drops, triggering cortisol and adrenaline (the fight-or-flight hormone) to release in the blood in an effort to rebalance your blood sugar.

The release of cortisol can cause aggression. Low blood sugar may interfere with higher brain functions that are supposed to help us control impulses and regulate our primitive drives and behavior.

Shocking right? Adding a snack between lunch and dinner rather than trying to "save your calories" for dining out could be the difference between someone sleeping on the couch versus getting physically romantic and falling asleep together.

On the flip side, if you're fueling your body correctly, eating balanced meals or snacks when you're hungry and stopping when you're full, you'll likely be more alert and have more patience and think more clearly.

The human brain demands a constant supply of about 20% of our total calorie daily needs. What we eat directly affects our brain's structure and functionality, and, ultimately, our mood. If you're under fueling calorically or nutritionally, you'll likely feel lackluster.

The International Society for Nutritional Psychiatry Research advocates for nutritional medicine to be considered a mainstream element of psychiatric practice. According to them, a whole-food diet consisting of higher intakes of vegetables, fruits, seafood, whole grains, lean meats, nuts and legumes, with the limiting processed foods, is more likely to defend against most mental health disorders. I'm not saying a balanced diet can solve all mental health struggles, but it can help.

Studies have also shown probiotics help reduce anxiety levels and perceptions of stress while improving mental outlook. However, more research is needed on probiotics before specific supplement recommendations can be used therapeutically. In the meantime, it may be beneficial to ingest fermented foods containing live, active cultures, such as kimchi, miso, sauerkraut, kombucha and yogurt.

When we're less stuck in our feelings, we're more present to opportunities in life. We try things that our suffering minds may have told us "we're not capable" of achieving. We prove to ourselves we can do what we put our mind to, which yields confidence followed by happiness.

GUT HEALTH

If you've ever "gone with your gut" to make a decision or felt "butterflies in your stomach" when you get nervous, you're likely getting signals from an unexpected source: Your *second* brain. Hidden in the digestive system walls, this "brain in your gut" is revolutionizing medicine's understanding of the links between digestion, mood, health and even the way you think.

Scientists call this little brain the enteric nervous system (ENS), and it's not so small. The ENS is two, thin layers of more than 100 million nerve cells lining your gastrointestinal (GI) tract stretching from the esophagus to the rectum.

Delving even deeper into the science, about 95% of serotonin (the neurotransmitter that helps regulate sleep, appetite and moods and inhibits pain) is produced in the GI tract. The GI tract is lined with millions of neurons and is highly influenced by the microbiome. The microbiome protects the intestinal lining against toxins and harmful bacteria, limits inflammation, improves the bioavailability of nutrients and activates neural pathways that travel directly between the gut and the brain.

But if you're restricting your intake by cutting out whole food groups or saying "screw it" and eating most foods out of a box and rarely eating vegetables, then your gut won't do its job as effectively. Research has shown a diet rich in plants (whole grains, fruits, vegetables, nuts and seeds) and soluble fiber to be beneficial for human health by promoting more diverse and stable microbial systems. And the more variety the better, which is why a rigid "clean eating" plan and an extreme calorie deficit doesn't work for your gut health or mental health in the long run.

IMMUNE FUNCTION

Inside the gut are about 100-trillion live microorganisms that promote normal GI function, protect the body from infection and regulate metabolism and the mucosal immune system. In fact, 75% of your immune system lies there, which is another reason why the quality of your food matters.

Inside every macronutrient is a micronutrient. These micronutrients, or vitamins and minerals, play a significant role in our overall health. Although deficiencies are rare due to technological advances of fortification, an imbalanced diet will result in suboptimal levels causing symptoms such as fatigue, bleeding gums, joint pain and even cognitive impairment.

When someone feels a cold coming on, they run to the drug store to load up on supplements. Vitamin C and zinc are the most popular purchases due to their ability to fight against compounds that damage the body and reduce infection. And it's true, Vitamin C, zinc, plus other micronutrients like vitamins A, D and E, and minerals like calcium and magnesium are capable of helping you prevent or treat illnesses.

But the part they are missing is they'd be much better off consuming foods with these nutrients already in them. Without eating nutrient-dense foods regularly, they are at a greater risk for developing chronic and acute diseases, whether they take the supplements or not.

Unfortunately, if you grew up in the '80s, you likely grew up fearing fat, keeping it low in your diet, thinking that was the healthy thing to do. But it wasn't. Because some essential micronutrients are fat-soluble, meaning the body can't absorb the nutrient without fat being present. And like previously discussed, a diet high in Omega-3 fats will help reduce inflammation, which is the root cause of most diseases.

Eat the rainbow. Variety is key. Aim to consume two to three servings of fruit per day and four to five servings of vegetables per day, and all different colors throughout the week to lessen your chances of contracting an acute illness or developing a chronic disease.

Water-soluble vitamins: B vitamins and vitamin C	Functions: Their main job is to produce energy, but they also help prevent cell damage from metabolic stress and are needed to create red blood cells	Good food sources: Whole grains, eggs, leafy greens (such as spinach), fish, lean meat, citrus fruits and bell peppers
Fat-soluble vitamins: Vitamins A, D, E and K	Functions: Protect vision, strengthen the immune system, support blood clotting and provide antioxidants to fight inflammation	Good food sources: Leafy greens, almonds, sweet potatoes, milk and soybeans
Microminerals: Microminerals are common minerals like calcium, phosphorus, magnesium, sodium and potassium	Functions: Maintain muscle and bone strength and control blood pressure	Good food sources: Milk products, leafy greens, black beans, lentils, bananas and fish (such as salmon)
Trace minerals: Iron, manganese, copper, zinc and selenium	Functions: Help with feeding oxygen to muscles, supporting nervous system function, healing wounds and defending cells against damage from stress	Good food sources: Oysters, spinach, pecans, peanuts and cashews

Chart created and adapted from Harvard Medical School

BEHAVIOR MODIFICATION

Now that you know diet quality, the quantity of food and how much physical activity and sleep someone gets impacts their weight, let's discuss ways to support them. And I don't mean temporarily, because anything you do temporarily will only produce temporary results, and I want you to have and feel the benefits for the rest of your life.

To do that, we need to shift to behavior modification to develop healthier habits because, like Aristotle put so nicely, "We are what we repeatedly do."

PHYSICAL ACTIVITY

There are ways to counter a sedentary lifestyle. I would recommend working your way up to the national guidelines of 150 minutes of aerobic exercise and two strength training sessions per week, with structured workouts. I understand that goal may be daunting for currently inactive people, leading them to forego exercising because they feel they'll never be able to meet these recommendations.

Fortunately, in 2018, the U.S. Department of Health and Human Services Physical Activity Guidelines changed physical activity recommendations by eliminating the minimum time requirement of at least 10 minutes per session and switched to key messaging focused on "something is better than nothing." Now promoting high-intensity incidental physical activity (HIIPA), or "any activity part of one's daily living that is not done with the purpose of recreation or health and requires no sacrifice of discretionary time."

Here's how you can increase your HIIPA:

- Take the stairs instead of the elevator and try to increase stepping speed for several steps at a time
- Park further in the parking lot when walking from the car to the store to increase the duration
- Carry your groceries rather than using a cart
- Walk to your job or an errand if able and walk fast enough to increase heart rate or breathing rate (include longer strides and try to pump your arms)
- Turn chores like cleaning, mopping, vacuuming, dusting, gardening, sweeping and raking leaves into a race by periodically speeding up movements for at least 10 seconds. Gradually increase the length of time of more intense movements to 30 seconds or a minute at a time
- Instead of watching children and pets play, move with them, playing chase or doing squats to pick up toys or play games
- Add a short lunchtime walk at work or dance when you hear your favorite song
- Volunteer for a cause you care about that encourages movement on a regular basis. Examples include dog walking at an animal shelter, working at museums and nonprofit organizations as a walking tour guide or cleaning up litter for local environmental organizations

The idea of using activities one is already doing as part of everyday life is much more realistic and achievable for most people. Coincidentally, as you increase your fitness with HIIPA, your interest in planned exercise also may increase. At the end of the day, do what you enjoy. The more you like what you're doing, the more likely you will continue to do it, which is how behavior modification turns into a habit.

Now that you've identified what's important to you and why, we can begin to build a roadmap to achieve your goals.

But in order to create a roadmap, we don't just need to know where we're going and how to get there. We need to know the challenges on the road ahead, which can include everything from highway hazards to wrong turns.

In the next chapter, we're going to identify some of the most common mistakes people make and talk about how not to make them. When it comes to your diet, knowing what not to do is sometimes more important than knowing what you should be doing.

CHAPTER 7

WILL THIS LAST PAST
THE HONEYMOON PHASE?

"A great relationship doesn't happen because of the
love you had in the beginning, but how well you
continue building love until the end."

- Unknown

Every relationship is the greatest relationship you've ever been in for the first three months. It's the so-called honeymoon phase -- the period during which everything seems right, nothing seems wrong and each and every moment you spend together feels like an explosion of joy.

Also called limerence[20], the honeymoon phase is often comprised of intense longing, lust and love. During those first few months, it seems like you're happier than you've ever been. You're floating on a cloud. Your heart is full. Your body aches for them. Your texts are a sea of emojis.

During this phase, you're also the least objective and possibly stupidest you'll ever be. OK, that may be a bit much, but only a bit.

The honeymoon phase makes us act a little silly because it's oh-so-good. You're both on your best behavior, keeping your less desirable habits tucked away in your respective closets.

---

[20] Coined by Dorothy Tennov in the late 1970s, "limerence" is used among researchers who study relationships.

You don't leave your towels on the floor; they always do the dishes. Every intimate encounter is hot, passionate and frequent, so you're both feeling attractive.

Limerence is a combination of both physiological and psychological events. On the physiological side, you've got the biochemical bonding that happens when two people have frequent sex: The rush of endorphines, the mix of pheromones and the release of oxytocin (the hormone responsible for pair-bonding). On the psychological side, you've got everything from the bliss of reciprocal attraction and desire to the intoxicating novelty of getting to know someone to the undeniable reality that both people are putting their best foot forward.

In short, it's a recipe for ignoring the signs. Limerence is a powerful experience. It can be a trancelike state during which you see everything in a positive light.

And why not? During that time, things are usually going quite well. So well, in fact, it can be nearly impossible to believe this person isn't *the one*, and that things will stay *this good* forever.

We overlook the little things because we're so focused on the passion. It's not until the hormonal-driven euphoria dies down that we begin to look more objectively at the other person and the relationship.

And that's when things get real …

This *same* thing happens when it comes to your nutrition.

Just like when we're in a new relationship with a person and can't stop talking about them, we probably do the same thing when we start a new diet. Everyone knows we're dating someone just like everyone knows we're trying keto.

Everything works at first. Right now, it's easy to adhere to the diet because it's going so well! The weight is falling off, and we suddenly believe keto was the answer all along. In reality, whether we were doing keto or paleo or just about any diet for that matter, it isn't because of the diet itself. As explained before, maintaining a calorie deficit does the trick.

But when things start to sour -- whether in a relationship or a new nutrition plan -- we feel like we have to stick with it. We declared it to everyone that we knew that this was going to be *the* one.

We all desperately want to stop the search. We want to be done having to lose weight just like we want to be done having to look for our partner. As a result, we settle into something that isn't right for us. We start to make excuses because, now that you have someone, you'll ignore things that are normally a deal breaker for you.

I can't even tell you how many second chances I gave to the guys who ghosted me all because I really wanted to be *wanted*. I convinced myself they deserved another chance when, really, it was clear they didn't. I ignored the warning signs because I was so full of hope I wouldn't have to be single anymore. People would stop asking me if I was seeing someone because I was at least dating, even if it wasn't the *right* guy. Just like people stopped critiquing me for being overweight as long as I told them I was working out and seemingly trying to *do something* about it.

We make excuses and try to convince ourselves that it's supposed to be hard so we lean into the difficulty of the diet or the relationship because they both take work in order to succeed, right?

But it's only been three months, and it shouldn't be hard within the first three months. Studies show motivation lasts for the first four to eight weeks of a diet. Then, after that, you have to put in more effort to stay on track. And since results are coming more slowly now, the desire to keep trying runs out as well. To add to that, things are no longer fun. It's gotten *real*, my friends.

As the saying goes, the honeymoon is *over*.

♥ ♥ ♥

NOTHING IS INHERENTLY BAD

If used correctly, everything has value. Even the practices I'd personally never recommend can, in some contexts, be beneficial for some people. As someone with a Bachelors in Science and a Masters in Nutrition, I believe in experimentation. I'm not against fad diets, fasting or counting points across the board. All of these experiences have value.

But when there are extreme claims (like not eating carbs is a lifestyle change), it bothers me because you don't see what I see. You only see the highlights.

You see Sally losing 30 pounds in two months, holding her XXL pant size next to her now-slimmer waist, but you rarely see the aftermath.

You don't usually hear her thoughts of feeling trapped by the diet, fearful to eat anything outside the plan. You don't hear the shame in her voice as she shares how upset she is for "being weak" and "feeling like a failure," for regaining the weight (and then some). That's the perspective I see too often.

Those are the clients who come to me, and I do everything in my power to remind them that deviating from those plans does not mean they lack will power. Because these diets are *not* meant to be followed for a lifetime (even when advertised otherwise).

Counting points and tracking calories can have merit when used with the right intentions.

When you treat them like an experiment, they can teach you a lot. So ask questions, do research, construct a hypothesis, set a goal, test it, analyze it, draw conclusions and make modifications based on the observations you've gathered.

Check in with your body. Ask yourself what foods felt good to eat and which ones didn't. Pay attention to your hunger cues, mood, bowel movements and energy.

Adjust as needed, and then try another method if needed, but understand one method is not superior to all others, and they're not meant to follow forever. Some people don't know how to eat if they aren't on a diet because they can't trust themselves, so they go on another diet. Just because you didn't follow one diet perfectly doesn't mean you can't take a portion of what *did* work for you and leave the rest behind until you've found *your* diet rather than constantly being *on* a diet. You need to commit to a *true* lifestyle change.

Some programs claim whatever results you achieve through it will remain after you've completed it. But the truth is, if you want to keep the results, you'll have to stay on the diet.

But when you're instructed to *only* drink shakes and eat bars, shovel down one plate of real food, cut out carbs, significantly restrict your intake and *not* exercise, it's only a matter of time before you feel like crap. You'll either stop doing it and gain all the weight back, or you're going to stick to it but be miserable.

We all have a diet, but you don't need to be on a diet to lose weight or be healthy. We just need to find the right balance for us.

♥ ♥ ♥

WHY IT WON'T LAST PAST THE HONEYMOON PHASE

At the start of something new, things are moving fast; progress is happening. Everything feels simple, and that makes it easy to miss (or ignore) the warning signs. When you've got rose-colored glasses on, red flags just look like regular, ol' flags.

What happens when the novelty fades? No matter how effective your diet is for the first three months, it's probably gonna taper off, and you can't live your whole life in your living room eating out of Tupperware. At some point, you've got to rejoin the world.

There are so many trends and fad diets out there that it would take a whole other book for me to write about them all. In this section, I've decided to share with you some popular phrases and eating styles I think are worth discussing. Please refer back to the fad diet chart in Chapter 4 to truly know if something will last past the honeymoon phase.

THE KETOGENIC DIET

Despites its popularity, most credible Registered Dietitians (RDs) aren't going to advise you to do The Ketogenic Diet unless you've been diagnosed with epilepsy or a serious neurological condition that warrants it.[21]

If you haven't caught on by now, carbs are *not* the enemy, and extreme restriction is rarely the answer. It's part of the problem.

But for argument's sake, let's pretend limiting your carbohydrate intake to fewer than 50 grams per day was practical and easy to apply: You're OK with giving up pizza with your friends, pasta with family and the occasional bagel for breakfast, indefinitely. Let's imagine you were fine with giving up fresh fruit as a snack, rice with your favorite stir-fry, hot cereal on cold winter mornings and ice cream on a hot summer day.

Let's pretend the initial drop in weight (which, for the record, is usually water weight due to the low carbo-*hydrate* intake), was enough motivation to keep you going. Would you stop when the brain fog started? When you begin feeling fatigued or nauseous? How about constipation? All of these are symptoms of the "keto flu," the result of the body's rapid excretion of sodium and fluids as carbohydrates are restricted.

I'm not sure why you would be, but let's imagine you *were* OK with all of that. You'd likely be advised to change your diet eventually due to either a nutrient deficiency or elevated cholesterol, which is a common result of excessive saturated fat and lack of soluble fiber intake.

---

[21] The reason behind this is because carbohydrates trigger the brain. Source: https://www.todaysdietitian.com/newarchives/0119p26.shtml

Think of me like your best friend who warned you about the person you wanted to date. You could go out with them and end up disappointed when things don't work out -- as your best friend predicted -- or you can skip the part when things don't work out by taking their advice, and trusting they had your best interests at heart.

As your best friend, this is what keto can teach you without having to go through the ups and downs of it: Carbohydrates from sugar-laden foods are not the same as carbohydrates from whole grains, starchy vegetables, beans, legumes and fruit.

Restricting all carbs is not necessary, but choosing more of the right types is. That combined with limiting added sugar and not excluding it completely is what can help you lose weight *healthily*.

MEAL PLANS

There are many things in life we can't control. Fortunately, what we eat is typically not often one of them.

For this reason, our desire for rigid meal plans is often heightened in times of stress, chaos and uncertainty.

In my teens, I spent hours going through magazines looking for the "perfect" plan. I'd get super excited and convince myself *this* was how I'd lose the weight *once and for all.* But, it didn't take long before that excitement faded. Mere days later, I'd be eating a box of cookies, judging myself for not adhering to the plan. Why couldn't I just be OK with eating egg whites and vegetables everyday?

Fortunately, as I got older, I got wiser. I wasn't the issue, and neither were the cookies. It was eating the entire box of cookies after no longer being able to ignore my hunger cues all day. I was trying to follow something that wasn't realistic for me (or most people for that matter).

Additionally, the lack of flexibility was contributing to the extreme inconsistencies, making me feel more out of control, which was the one thing I was trying to fix in the first place.

To find balance in my eating habits, I had to stop focusing on how food might make me *look* and focus more on how it made me *feel*, and that couldn't be found in a magazine.

So when you find yourself thinking "I need a meal plan," what you really need is to have a reliable way to track food intake without it becoming your entire life.

One such method is to take photos of your food. This is typically the least stressful and most helpful, but it's up to you to pick the tracking tool you think you're most likely to keep up with.

Each week, review the foods you ate that made you feel satisfied and energized versus those that didn't. The foods that made you feel good become part of your "go-to" options and those that didn't get swapped out.

Notice how I said "swapped" not "taken" out. Swaps are healthy alternatives, which allow for flexibility in the plan. Removing foods is about restriction. Having substitutions shows you the many different ways to nourish your body, which is why your plan shouldn't look like anyone else's. Also, swapping instead of taking out means if you're out with your friends and don't see a typical swap option on the menu, you won't guilt yourself for hours over having to eat a "forbidden" food.

At the end of the day, make a plan to swap out anything that doesn't make you feel your best, both mentally and physically.

Here's a step-by-step process of how you can create your own meal plan:

1. Track your food and beverage intake for a week. Be honest. Include portions and amounts. It's OK if you didn't make the best choices. That's exactly what we need to see.

2. Assess what went well and what didn't. Then ask *why*. The why will tell you what to do next. For example: If you ate a balanced breakfast because you prepared it the night before but overate at dinner because you forgot to pack lunch and snacks, you now know you need to prep more.

3. Repeat steps one and two for two weeks, and start highlighting your "go-to" staple items.

4. Write a weekly menu, plotting out your breakfast, lunch, dinner and snacks for the week using your staples. When planning your meals, aim to have healthy choices from at least three food groups. When planning your snacks, make at least one snack nutritious or protein-rich to hold you over in between meals. This can help prevent you from overeating at night. Consider rotating a few options after each week so you don't get bored with it. Review it daily to check if modifications are needed based on activities. (Examples include higher training days at the gym, traveling, dinners out with friends.)

5. Be patient. If you're looking for a meal plan because you're not seeing progress in your health goals, you probably haven't tried this long enough. Try it consistently for three weeks (weekends included).

You don't have to do this forever, but this process will get you past the honeymoon phase. Once you know your staples, you can trust your cravings and hunger cues more.

EVERYTHING IN MODERATION

As someone who preaches a balanced diet with flexibility, you're probably surprised to read I don't believe *everything* should be consumed moderately. In fact, I think this philosophy is the exact reason many people struggle to make progress, consistently.

Are you proactively defining what moderation means to you or are you falling victim to moments of temptation, using it as a crutch in order to not stick to what you said you were going to do?
For instance:

- Do you want to limit how many alcoholic drinks you have per week or do you want to drink alcohol whenever it's offered to you, ignoring the goal you set?

- Are you eating ice cream only when the occasional craving kicks in or do you eat it every night just because your partner is?

- Are you eating a small portion of the nachos your friends ordered or are you inhaling half the platter because you've been "good"[22] all week

---

[22] Many people associate eating healthy with being on their best behavior, but choosing to eat one way or another doesn't change your worth or value as a person. Whatever you choose to eat does not make you good or bad.

We all have different likes, dislikes and goals. Establish yours clearly and decide what variety of choices fit within that definition. From there, you can build your own version of "moderation" and truly find balance in your eating habits.

♥ ♥ ♥

KNOWING WHEN TO PUSH PAST THE HONEYMOON PHASE

Commitment isn't easy, but it's a lot harder when it's surrounded by uncertainty. I've finally learned when it's protected by clear boundaries and expectations, commitment comes naturally when it's in line with your values.

When my current boyfriend and I met, we both had been hurt in the past. We were cautious, almost jaded and were unsure who we could trust.

Being together felt great. The connection was real, and the conversations were effortless.

That old impulse to dive headfirst into a relationship was there, but then doubt crept in, fueled by prior experiences. What if things fell apart? What if we got hurt again?

So we moved slowly.

Historically, I'd go on two dates with someone and suddenly have a new boyfriend, but with him, it was different. We dated for six months before deciding to commit to one another. Half a year of calls and texts, low-key date nights and deep talks led to this.

Sitting here now, it's easy to look back and laugh at how

nervous we were, but then we'd be missing the lesson. Hindsight is 20/20, and those six months laid the foundation for the special relationship we have now.

You've probably experienced a similar situation in your health journey. You've invested time, effort and energy into a plan that didn't work. You were so excited about it. You went all in right away, but then you couldn't follow it at parties or stick to it when you were with your family. Trying to comply became more exhausting than not, so you gave up.

Do that same song-and-dance enough times, and it's easy to become weary. But, just like relationships, it's not a "failure" if you learn something, which is why you can't stop trying.

No one who stopped trying ever got what they wanted.

The key is to let the lessons from your past guide you *without* letting the pain from your past hold you back. It's time to stop throwing "caution to the wind" and graduate to "cautious optimism."

Instead of rearranging your entire life to fit into the hot new diet trend, go slowly. Try a few things out. See what works for you. If you see progress without it overshadowing the rest of your life, dive in a little deeper.

Both healthy living and relationships take work, but neither should consume you. A little bit of effort every day goes a long way.

That's how you find a diet (and relationship) that works for you in the long-run.

But if you encounter a new diet, and you're curious if it falls under the fad diet category, here are some flowcharts to help you decipher that.

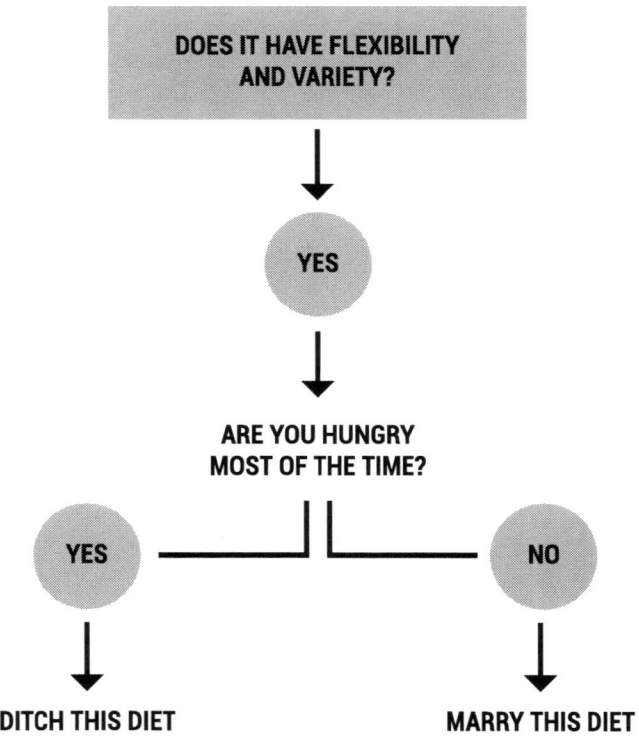

DOES IT HAVE FLEXIBILITY AND VARIETY?

YES

ARE YOU HUNGRY MOST OF THE TIME?

YES — NO

DITCH THIS DIET

MARRY THIS DIET

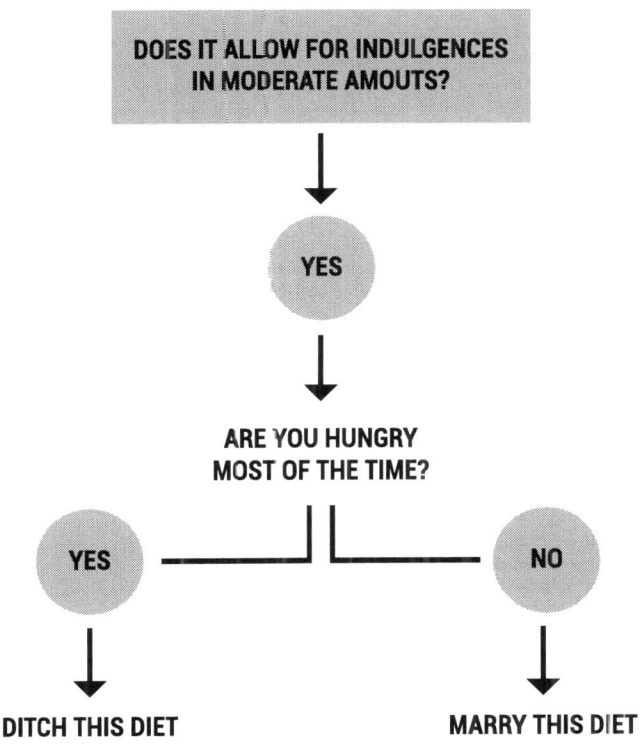

DOES IT ALLOW FOR INDULGENCES
IN MODERATE AMOUTS?

YES

ARE YOU HUNGRY
MOST OF THE TIME?

YES

NO

DITCH THIS DIET

MARRY THIS DIET

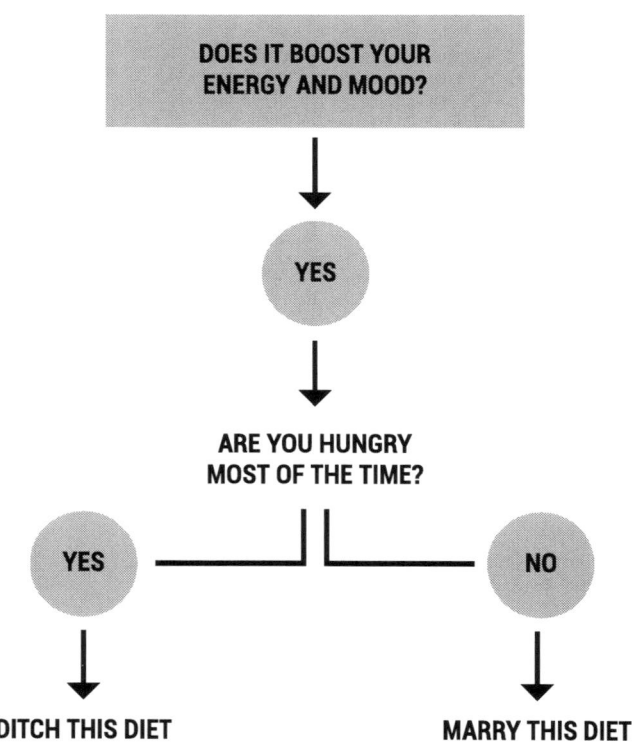

CHAPTER 8

DO I EVEN LIKE THIS?

"Please don't settle. Not in a job you hate, not in a town where you don't feel at home, not with friendships that aren't real, and especially not with love."

- Marisa Donnelly, self help author

It's 10:15 at night. You've had *the* longest day and are fighting to keep your eyelids from closing. You think to yourself, "I need to go to bed," but then you turn to your partner and remember this is when you spend time together.

His eyes are glued to the TV, watching sports highlights on ESPN when you realize what used to be a weekly thing has now become a daily routine.

In the beginning of the relationship, you looked forward to nights like this. Watching *Sportscenter* was an opportunity to learn about how different games were played, hear stories about his high school football days and then catch up during the commercials about the newest drama at his office.

But now it seems like you haven't watched a TV show *you* wanted to watch in ages, and the conversations between you two have changed from getting to know each other to, "What should we do for dinner?"

Even that's become a pattern. You aren't even sure why he asks anymore, since 90% of the time you settle on ordering from *his* favorite restaurant.

Too exhausted from a mentally draining day to care, you end up eating a meal you didn't even want, trying to satisfy a craving that has nothing to do with food in the first place.

As a result, your subconscious searches for ways to compensate.

Despite the many mornings you tell yourself you're done overeating, you once again find yourself surrounded by crumpled candy wrappers and an empty sleeve of cookies.

Anyone on the outside looking in could tell what's going on here: You're eating to mask the deeper, emotional cravings for connection, communication, affection and love.

You're knee-deep in a relationship that no longer provides what you need emotionally. If only you could get it back. The magic. The mystery. The novelty. Instead, you stay in the relationship, trying to fill the void with a bag of chips.

But the good news is you can regain some objectivity with a simple, but not-so-easy, question. It's a question that cuts to the very heart of *any* relationship -- whether with a person, with food, with a diet or with yourself.

"Do I even like this?"

THAT TIME I WAS A VEGETARIAN ... AND THEN A VEGAN ... AND THEN A GLUTEN-FREE VEGAN

I spent most of my college years bloated and hungry. I'd gone "all in" on being a vegetarian, convinced it was the *only* way to be healthy.

Over time, my progress slowed, so naturally, I decided I needed to make some changes. "If being vegetarian is good," I reasoned, "being vegan must be better." It was more restrictive, eliminated more foods and made my life harder in every way -- so it had to be the right move.

My decision to transition into veganism happened to coincide with Lent, the 40-day period leading up to the Easter holiday during which many Christians traditionally abstain from eating meat on certain days to reflect on Jesus' sacrifices and fasting. Growing up Greek Orthodox, honoring God is pretty much the only acceptable reason to give up meat in my family, and I knew they would need to be supportive in order for this to work. I told everyone I was experimenting with veganism as a religious practice, but really, I was hoping to lose more weight.[23]

Except, when Jesus resurrected on that Easter Sunday, I never broke my fast. I decided to keep all animal products out of my diet, insisting I felt *great* while the hunger and bloat increased.

When I graduated college, my belly continued to swell, and the discomfort became impossible to ignore. At that time, the gluten-free diet was pretty popular. There were scientific articles stating that, although the gluten-free diet was primarily for those diagnosed with Celiac disease (an autoimmune disease which causes a wheat allergy), there are some people who reported a significant decrease in symptoms like bloating when removing gluten from their diet. Something else to remove from my diet? Perfect. Naturally, I tried it.[24]

---

[23] In fairness to me, this is not uncommon. For many Christians I know, "I'm giving it up for Lent" was a common refrain in their household, with family members declaring they'd stopped eating sweets or carbs or alcohol. While the symbolic sacrifice of abstaining from something you like is certainly in line with the spirit of the practice, the Lenten tradition is often used to kick-start or support a diet of some sort. Diet culture has permeated every facet of our lives that it shows itself even in our religious traditions.
[24] Hindsight is 20/20.

In this situation, I'm fortunate I did cut out the gluten, because the bloating happened a lot less often. But now, I was gluten free *and* vegan, severely reducing the types of foods I was allowing myself to eat.

My diet, once a robust selection of foods, was reduced to fruits, vegetables, peanut butter and tofu. While this is certainly better than those late nights spent gorging on Oreos snatched from my grandparents' pantry as a kid, it had its own set of complications.

I continued to feel hungry all of the time. My family also couldn't keep up with my dietary changes and got more concerned or annoyed, depending on the day. They had supported me through Lent, as my veganism was focused on deepening my relationship with God, but once that had passed, they simply couldn't wrap their heads around the idea I wasn't going to go back to eating meat. It was just like the scene from *My Big Fat Greek Wedding:* "What do you mean you don't eat no meat?"

After months of trying to talk me into eating lamb, they began to make a conscious effort to have veggie burgers in the freezer or whole grain pasta for me.

Unfortunately, as a gluten-free vegan, those options weren't even foods I could eat either. They were so accommodating, how could I tell them I couldn't eat the pasta they made me and that the veggie burgers they bought contained an ingredient my body couldn't tolerate?

In an effort to hide the severity of my dietary restrictions, I'd make do, often leaving family gatherings having eaten all the carrots and hummus from the crudite platter, two to three plates of salad and all the fruit for dessert. Sounds healthy, looks healthy, but it wasn't. My stomach was physically filled to capacity, but psychologically, I wanted more.

After countless get-togethers, something finally clicked in me: Never feeling satisfied is not how healthy eating should feel. So I began to explore what I was missing.

The answer was right under my nose the whole time, a message I preached on my brand new Tips With Toni blog: Balance. It was time for me to practice what I preached and explore what worked for *me*, regardless of what articles and trends said.

That's when I started adding animal protein again, but this time, more slowly. It became glaringly obvious that on the days I incorporated more animal protein, my cravings, hunger and bloating decreased.

I continued to make tiny tweaks. A bit more protein. Keep the gluten out. Eat larger meals less often. I ate more on days I went to the gym. And so on.

In the end, it took me six years to learn I didn't need to be a vegetarian or a vegan or a gluten-free vegan to make vegetables the star of the dish.

Experimentation and observation aren't fast processes, but things took a lot longer for me than they should have, and I want them to go more quickly for you.

This is why you need to ask yourself the question: "Do I even like this?" and be brutally honest with your answer.

FINDING YOUR MAGIC

In Nicholas Sparks' classic romantic novel *The Notebook*, a rich girl named Allie falls desperately in love with Noah, a mill worker. Due to their social and economic differences, her family doesn't approve. Noah goes off to war, and Allie moves on. She ends up getting engaged to another man, Lon Hammond, Jr; a well-established lawyer whose income and social standing make him a better (or, at least, a more family-approved) match for Allie.

Allie was *content* in their relationship. Lon treated her well. She had financial security, and she even saw herself starting a family with him. But deep down, she knew the future she pictured with Lon wasn't what she truly *wanted*. She felt in her gut that passion was missing.

That became apparent when she realized she hadn't painted in years, something she loved and used to do all of the time. It was then she realized the *thing* she was missing was Noah. She loved Lon, but she was still *in love* with Noah.

Staying with her fiancé was safe, but, in the end, she decides to upgrade her *good enough* relationship for something magical.

If it hadn't been for the connection with Noah, Allie probably would have settled for mediocrity. I think this is a lesson we all need. Just because something works, doesn't mean it's *working*. Sure, you can have a job that pays well, your co-workers are decent, the hours are flexible and the work is semi-inspiring, but if it's not fully aligned with your greater purpose, then you'll almost always wonder: "What if?"

That describes me at my last job before moving forward with

my nutrition coaching business full time. I wasn't *unhappy*. I was grateful. I was respected at work. People looked up to me. My commute was an 8-minute drive. I could go out for lunch. I had my own office. I was basically my own boss, but I knew I could do more and be more. I knew I wanted to write this book, do my first TEDx talk, earn more money, have even more flexibility and make a deeper impact. That's when I chose to swap out *good* for *great*. I was leaving stability for unpredictability, but it was a chance I needed to take.

The same Notebook-esque mentality happens to us in many facets of life. One of my clients, Amanda, hated running, but she lived in a town filled with avid runners. And not just people who jogged on the treadmill. We're talking ultra-marathoners. Wanting to make friends and "fit in," Amanda took up running. She had heard about the "runner's high" people got, so she chased that dragon.

But the longer she ran, the more she hated it. She dreaded every time she put on her sneakers. She kept upping her distances until she felt like she could "brag" about it during conversations. She eventually ran a half marathon with many of her friends, including her new boyfriend whom she (can you predict this?) bonded with over their mutual running regimen. Once she crossed that finish line, she enjoyed the attention and the celebratory beer afterward, but she wasn't truly happy. She was trying so hard to be a part of something larger, she ignored the fact that every foot fall made her sad.

Finally, she decided to step out. She found a workout routine that still made her feel athletic without being so running-centric. And guess what? Her friends still enjoyed her and her boyfriend still liked her because she exuded the happiness she had been seeking in the first place. She found the magic she had been looking for, and it all came from listening to her gut.

COMPROMISE VS. SACRIFICE

Five years ago, if you'd asked me what commitment meant, I would've told you it means never giving up *no matter what.*

I would've told you it meant sacrifice and putting forth maximum amounts of effort to *make* it work. Although some of that may be true, I was missing the most important part: Sometimes it just isn't worth holding on to.

Without that realization, I stayed in relationships longer than I should've and tried diets that did more harm than good.

I was so fixated on finding *the one* or losing 20 pounds, I was blind to the warning signs begging me to reassess and redirect my path. But after a handful of tumultuous break-ups and fights with the scale, I couldn't ignore the red flags any longer.

If I wanted to find happiness both in myself and with someone else, I needed to define what actually mattered to me.

Before my current partner and I decided to be together, we had an honest conversation about how we expected to be treated. We agreed if, at any point, we felt mistreated, we'd immediately communicate about it. We wouldn't let our emotions build up, and we'd address things directly.

The purpose of our relationship is to help each other grow, both mentally and emotionally. We're well aware if either of us breaks our promise of supporting one another, we'd hold each other accountable. And after that, if it keeps happening, we won't be blindsided that it's time to split.

The same goes for my nutrition journey. I'm committed to

being the healthiest version of myself, but if that requires sacrificing my mental health, I know I need to find a better way.

Because compromise and sacrifice both require effort and energy, they can feel similar, but they're not the same. In a compromise, the work you put in is reciprocated. There's a positive feedback loop, which makes it worth it. Sacrifice, on the other hand, feels exhausting and is often at the expense of your happiness.

Now, I know commitment doesn't have to be hard. It just has to be agreed upon and clearly defined.

So many people are following a diet because they're terrified if they're not following something, they'll gain weight.

Taking some time off from following a structured plan doesn't mean you're going to gain weight, just like deleting dating apps for a few months doesn't mean you'll wind up a crazy cat lady. *(And that's coming from a cat lady)*

Sometimes, taking a step back is what we need to realize happiness doesn't depend on the number on the scale or whether or not we have a date lined up for Friday night.

Whether it's a date or a diet, the chances of finding exactly what works for you right off the bat are pretty slim. But while you may be disappointed, it's never a waste of your time as long as it teaches you something.

The second you realize that, it's time to ask yourself my next and final question, "What lessons did I learn from this?"

CHAPTER 9

WHAT LESSONS DID I
LEARN FROM THIS?

"Wisdom is the lesson you need,
right after you need it."

- *John Romaniello,* writer and entrepreneur

If you grew up in the '90s like me, then you know all about the ending of *Sex and The City* when -- after six season of the tumultuous, on-again-off-again relationship between protagonist Carrie Bradshaw and her recurring love interest Mr. Big -- they finally make it more official. Depending on whom you ask, you'll hear either excitement about this or disappointment. I fall into the latter camp. While most TV romances have a strong dose of will-they-won't-they energy to add some drama and suspense to the storyline, watching Carrie chase after someone with clear commitment and intimacy phobias was painful even by sitcom standards.

They break up twice over the course of two years, including Big's unforgivable jilting at the altar. I believe in forgiveness and all, but taking someone back after they embarrass you in front of your family and friends *on your wedding day* ... personally, I'm not sure I could have ever recovered from that.

Somehow, Carrie overlooks it and gives Big *yet another chance*. Watching "love" stories like this on TV and movies explains why we do what we do. They paint struggles in relationships as romantic and often heroic. As long as it works out in the end -- and, in these films, it always seems to -- then it was all worth it, no matter how painful or traumatic. If we take away the "happy ending" (pretend Carrie didn't end up with Big), does that make her less happy? What if the ending was she finally realized *she needed to stop trying to make something work that clearly didn't,* despite how much she loved him?

LESSON ONE:
FROM YO-YO DIET TO YOUR DIET

One of the more popular nutrition books over the past decade is *Whole30* by Dallas and Melissa Hartwig, which is essentially a comprehensive elimination diet. From a very simplistic angle, it could be considered a cleanse, but ultimately, it creates a reset as a testing ground to determine food sensitivities.

According to the website, *"The Whole30* is designed to change your life in 30 days—but it's not a diet, a detox, or a weight loss program. Think of it as a short-term *reset*, created to help you curb your cravings and bad habits, boost your metabolism, heal your digestive tract and calm your immune system."

Yet, it contains a laundry list of foods to *not* consume, from added sugar, (real or artificial) to alcohol in any form (not even for cooking), no grains (even whole), no legumes, dairy, preservatives, baked goods, junk foods or even treats with "approved" ingredients. Basically you can only eat meat, seafood, eggs, vegetables, fruit, natural fats, herbs, spices and seasonings.

In essence, Whole30, despite the insistence it's not a detox or a cleanse, labels about 95% of generally available foods as off-limits -- which sounds an awful lot like a detox to me.

Now, in fairness, if used properly, Whole30 is probably very effective at achieving its intent: Learning what foods don't work with your particular physiology. But the fact is, most people don't use it that way. Instead, it's often a hyper-restrictive kick-start used for quick weight loss, often as a prelude to another (slightly less) restrictive nutrition plan. This isn't the creators' fault, of course, but in a world influenced by diet culture, we need to have realistic expectations of how the tools we create will be used.

Due to its lack of supervision by a nutrition professional, those who try Whole30 typically stop following it for one of two reasons:

1. It's too restrictive, and they give up before the part where you're supposed to *slowly* add foods back in
2. They actually start to feel better, less bloated, with more energy and, terrified of backsliding, attempt to make the 30-day restriction a full-time practice, eventually cracking under the strain

In either case, the user experiences food guilt and develops fear of all of the foods they've eliminated. They associate grains, dairy, soy, nuts, sugar and *anything* processed as "bad" and stress over their diet more than before.

Many people do Whole30 and then go back to their old eating habits. Now, instead of yo-yoing with their weight, they yo-yo with elimination and extreme exposure. If you go from eliminating gluten, dairy, soy and nuts and then add them back in all at once, you'll likely experience gastrointestinal distress, which makes it difficult to identify which was the actual culprit of your gut issues or how much may be tolerable.

The *concept* behind Whole30 is a great example of how we should treat all diets and all nutrition plans. Most of them are going to last longer than 30 days and very few of them are going to be as strict, but the goal of every nutrition plan should be in part to determine what about this is making me successful.

The process you'll discover in this chapter uses *retrospective analysis*, which means even if you don't get the results you want from any particular diet, you get the *information* you need to make all subsequent nutrition plans more effective and help you make the right decisions going forward.

Whole30 is a microcosm of elimination and testing. Moreover, it's a framework that works better in theory than practice. You can get results, but what it's really doing is creating a strict container to help you identify what works and what doesn't. Whether or not I agree with Whole30 or not is irrelevant.

The point is that not *everything* works for *everyone*. Two people of nearly identical weight can go through the same nutrition plan and have wildly different results. Or, perhaps more confusingly, they can have similar results for vastly different reasons. Finally, even if they go through the same experience, they come out with different lessons.

LESSON TWO: SAME DIET, DIFFERENT DATA

One of the primary determinants for selecting a diet is proximal association. In other words, we often choose which diet we're going to follow based *not* on what seems like it might work for us, but rather because it seemingly worked for someone else we know. This often-overlooked piece of the puzzle creates a lot of issues.

You may have heard the phrase: "It's different for everybody, because every *body* is different." Nutrition professionals use this bit of clever wordplay to explain why some diets work better for some people than others.

Because no two bodies are alike, no single diet will have the same effect on them. People have different exercise habits, metabolisms, starting points, body compositions and genetic predispositions, just to name a few. Any one of those can shift the efficacy of a diet. In combination, the results can be drastic. And that's without even considering a host of non-physiological factors, from cultural preferences, work-life balance, schedule, socialization, family obligations and so forth.

In my dietetics practice, I see this all the time.

Before working with me, both Judy and Riley had tried WW (formerly known as Weight Watchers). They agreed it was effective for a short while, but they didn't want to count points their entire life and never really understood why certain things were unlimited while others weren't. They found it frustrating and confusing when the rules kept changing.

Similar to counting calories, if they ate too much in the beginning of the day, it would lead to feeling restricted at the end of the day, and instead of finding ways to modify or go over just a little bit, they'd toss it out the window, eat whatever and feel defeated. They never learned a way to eat outside of the system.

They both agreed tracking points was helpful in the

TRACKING TOOLS PROS AND CONS

PEN AND PAPER/ NOTES SECTION OF PHONE

PROS
- Able to write your mood before and after a meal and the time of day that you ate it
- Makes you think twice by bringing awareness to food choices
- Good if you prefer a physical tracking tool

TAKING PHOTOS OF YOUR FOOD

PROS
- Visualization of portion size
- Creates awareness of food consumed with less stress

USE YOUR INSTAGRAM ACCOUNT/ SOCIAL MEDIA PROFILE

PROS
- Potential to be inspired by other accounts
- Followers give you a sense of responsibility which can hold you accountable
- Easy to discover new healthy recipes and share photos of yours

DOWNLOAD A TRACKING APP

PROS
- Big database with convenient label-scanning option
- Includes a pie chart with the amount & percentage of protein, fat, and carbs consumed
- Micro-nutrient lists available to assess food quality
- Upgrade available to specify macro/micros. timing of meals, & modify day-to-day
- Can edit and plan for the following day and review previous days

TRACKING TOOLS PROS AND CONS

PEN AND PAPER/ NOTES SECTION OF PHONE

CONS
- Time consuming or inconvenient
- Under or over estimating the amount of food entered

TAKING PHOTOS OF YOUR FOOD

CONS
- Doesn't take into account the amount of calories or preparation methods used
- Underestimation of food actually consumed (May not take a picture of every tiny snack eaten)

USE YOUR INSTAGRAM ACCOUNT/ SOCIAL MEDIA PROFILE

CONS
- Hate comments
- Misinformation not regulated
- Conflicting views can make it confusing to sift through

DOWNLOAD A TRACKING APP

CONS
- Some user-generated calories/macros may be inaccurate
- Can become obsessive & interferes w/ quality of life
- Guessing entry, rather than weighing/measuring. Leads to inaccuracies
- Estimated calorie needs aren't 100% reliable & may lead to the "screw it" mentality (when goal is too low)

beginning, but what once felt easy to control eventually became the root of feeling out of control.

Knowing tracking is an important part to bring awareness to one's food choices, I encouraged them to track but in a less restrictive way.

In the beginning of working with me, I do this by instructing my clients to start taking photos of their meals. From there, I begin educating them about their choices and explaining how to balance their day and their plates and find ways to make small improvements to their usual food intake.

After a month or so of that, along with forming healthier habits around sleep, hydration, stress management and movement, Judy and Riley brought up the idea of "macro tracking."

Tracking your macros (short for macronutrients) is a more specific guide to ensure your body is getting everything it needs. It's similar to counting points, but with this, you learn each food and drink's face value and understand the flexibility and ability to modify meals or snacks based on what you were in the mood for that day.

Initially, both Judy and Riley loved their experience with tracking macros. They were losing weight and learning at the same time. They felt in control of their food choices because, for the first time, they understood the *why* behind it.

As the months passed, Judy started to feel trapped and didn't like the idea of having to count macros each day. She had lost a decent amount of weight and was happy with her progress, and we agreed to slowly remove the tracking. At that point, she had a deep understanding of how certain foods made her feel, what proper portions were and how to navigate social situations like going to a party or a restaurant without experiencing anxiety over what to eat.

Judy went from tracking seven days a week to only tracking on weekends, to only taking photos of food, to not tracking at all and depending fully on her hunger cues. She had her go-to meal and snack options and felt comfortable eating on a schedule. We agreed if her habits started to slip, she could always bring tracking back temporarily to reignite her momentum.

Riley, on the other hand, loved tracking her macros. Even after two years of working together, she still tracks them. She says it's like a puzzle. Through working together, she knows she can make her favorite ice cream fit while balancing out the remainder of her day, but to her, she said she likes *seeing* it. She understands if it ever gets to the point of food obsession, it's time to take a break.

At some point, tracking her macros made Judy feel trapped. Meanwhile, for Riley, it provided a sense of freedom. They both learned to listen to their bodies, no longer feeling restricted and worried about going over their calories or running out of points. They know tracking is a tool to help shape their diet compared to their old mindset of using tracking as *the* diet.

My goal with my clients is to help them come to an understanding of the things necessary for their success and their happiness. And, just like relationships, you usually have to find out what you do want by crossing off what you don't.

Looking back on past experiences is often the *only* way to do that.

SOMETIMES YOU NEED TO LEARN THE "HARD" WAY

Author and entrepreneur John Romaniello -- who's also one of my mentors and helped with the writing of this very book -- always says, "Experience is the bridge between knowledge and wisdom."

John's point is even when we *know* something, cognitive awareness isn't enough to get us to act on it. Most important lessons we learn oftentimes have to be learned by looking backward, and it's only after the experience we can gain the insight.

Not everyone will get the same lesson from the same experience. If you don't take the time to reflect and identify what you want to bring into your future and what you want to leave in the past, then you'll stay stuck jumping from diet to diet, never finding *the* one.

Which is why you always need to ask yourself: *"What lessons did I learn from this?"*

THE PROCESS OF INQUIRY

Actress Sasha Azevedo once said, "We can teach from experience, but we can't teach experience." For example, we might know better, but that doesn't mean we always *do* better. Because sometimes we need to *feel it* rather than *think it* to decipher what's best for us.

Some people learn by observing, but most of us learn by doing.

Like being warned to stay away from the "bad boy," hearing

about the downsides of fad diets, juice cleanses and detoxes may not be enough to keep you from trying them anyway. You may need to experience it yourself to be convinced.

Even if we acknowledge experience is the necessary ingredient to turn *knowledge* into *wisdom*, we've still got to do a little work to make sure we absorb the lesson.

In this regard, there is no better tool than self-reflection. This is what allows us to take stock of the experiences we've had and discern what we've learned.

To that end, below is a list of questions I want you to ask yourself before, during and after a diet or relationship didn't end in a way you expected:

WOULD YOU DO IT AGAIN? AND IF SO, WHAT WOULD YOU CHANGE?

Maybe you enjoyed calorie counting because it kept you aware of your food choices, prompted you to read nutrition facts labels, helped with portion control and allowed you to make substitutions you felt good about. But looking back, you realize you spent every Friday saving up your calories for an extra large dinner which bordered on binge eating. And even though you were able to get yourself back to tracking the following day (and still lost weight!), you hated feeling out of control.

Reflecting back, you saw why this kept happening: Your daily caloric intake was too low. You would go to bed hungry most nights, and, by the end of a long work week, you didn't have the mental vigor to resist anymore.

Using this feedback, you can change one of two things: You

can either adjust the calorie goal to reflect a refeed day[25] so you don't feel guilty about it or adjust the calories to be slightly higher each day to prevent feeling restricted.

WAS IT WORTH IT?

There are times where sacrifice is worth it. I reflect back to training for my very first half marathon when Saturdays were my long run days. Realizing drinking alcohol on Friday nights -- even if it were a single glass of wine -- would make my run feel sluggish the next morning, I made the choice to refrain from drinking socially, and I rarely stayed out late because my rest was important to me. After I crossed that finish line, I remember thinking it was so worth it. All of the runs I pushed myself to do beforehand, the early morning training sessions, the limited late nights out, it was all worth it because I did something I never thought I could do: Run 13.1 miles without stopping.

It's hard to know if something will be worth it without trying it, however, we can use our past to help us look into the future. For example, there was a period in my life when I considered training for a bikini competition. But after several sessions of self-examination (using questions like these), I never did. Because, even though I knew I'd feel proud of myself for doing it, I also knew I'd do irreversible damage to my mind and body. Considering my history of body dysmorphia and orthorexia, it would have only made things worse. To this day, I know I made a smart decision for me. It wouldn't have been worth it.

---

[25] A "refeed" is a planned adjustment in your diet during which you increase caloric intake for a day. This has a number of benefits, including a boost to recovery from workout and a psychological break from dieting.. This is something of which we need to be mindful, and for that reason, I recommend them with caution, and advise against more extreme versions, such as highly-restricted caloric intake offset by a no-holds-barred cheat day.

ONCE UPON A DIET

JOURNAL PROMPT WEEK AFTER, MONTH AFTER, 3-6 MONTHS AFTER, YEARS AFTER

Using reflective inquiry is most certainly helpful after an experience doesn't have the happy ending you longed for, but it can also be advantageous in the *middle* of an experience. If more people chose to ask questions during, they'd have a lot more happy endings.

Here are some questions to use:

- *Week after:* How is my mood? Energy? Bowel movements? Did I accomplish what I said I was going to (ex. 3 workouts, veggies at every meal, a gallon of water per day)?

- *Month after:* Same questions as the week after but add: How many weeks did I accomplish what I said I was going to?

- *3 months after:* Same questions as before but add: Am I closer to my goal than I was a month ago? Do I still like this? What needs to change?

- *6 months after:* Same as the previous checkpoints plus: Can I see myself doing this for another 6 months?

- *1 year after:* Same as all the previous check-ins but make sure to ask: Am I the same person I was a year ago? Did I grow, remain the same, or backslide into unhealthy habits? Does this plan still fit my lifestyle? Does this person still bring me the same excitement and joy?

WHAT PARTS DID YOU LIKE ABOUT IT THAT YOU'D TAKE WITH YOU IN YOUR NEXT RELATIONSHIP/DIET?

Wouldn't it be awesome if we could take all the good qualities from our former experiences -- whether it's an ex-partner or a diet you've ditched -- and put them together to make the perfect plan (or, better, a perfect partner)? I'll take the tall, dark and handsome from X, the good job and good family from Y, and the good sex and funny personality from Z, but leave the parts of them that left the toilet seat up, would "forget" to call and hated cats. I'd love to take the high protein from paleo, the ease of intermittent fasting and the focus on veggies from veganism but happily ditch the intense restriction from the first, the stressing about the clock from the second and the limited food selection from the third.

We can't always control who we fall for, but we *can* control who we look for. The law of attraction states you will get what you look for. So if you want a tall, dark and handsome man with a solid job and family life, who's good in bed, has a great sense of humor, loves cats, respects your feelings and remembers to put his dishes in the dishwasher, will him into existence. You may not get all of the above, but you just may get 90% of him.

Fortunately, you *can* control which of the nutrition plans you put into place. You can have a diet that puts both vegetables and protein at the center of every meal, has some easy-to-follow-guidelines that create structure without being restrictive and allow you to make progress without giving up all social dining, making it easier to follow through.

Here are some examples of taking the good and leaving the bad:

- If you enjoyed the meals you prepared on a previous diet, but they took too long to prepare, choose one per week rather than having to make a new one each day
- If you felt good eating more vegetables, fill half of your plate with them, rather than feeling like you can *only* eat them
- If you noticed you felt fuller and craved fewer sweets when you ate more protein, focus on incorporating a decent amount of protein at each meal

WHAT WOULD YOU MISS IF YOU DIDN'T DO IT/HAVE IT?

Define your non-negotiables. What are you not willing to give up? Have you heard you need to give up your favorite things like coffee and wine to be healthy?

I have, and if it were true, well, then I may be the unhealthiest person on this planet. A day without coffee would leave me absolutely miserable, and a week without wine would be a serious struggle.

There are so many diets out there that forbid things like coffee and alcohol, but why?

Sure, consuming excessive amounts of caffeine and alcohol cause harm to the body. But, did you know that 1 to 2 cups of coffee per day and a small amounts of alcohol per week can actually do a body good?

Unfortunately, diets only know how to talk in extremes, leaving you feeling guilty about a majority of your food choices, but it does not have to be all or nothing.

You can learn to enjoy your favorite foods in a balanced way.

Think of foods in terms of quality first then quantity second. Choose healthier options more often than not, and eventually, you'll develop a better diet overall.

There's no reason why you need to avoid your favorite things in order to be healthy, because there's no one food or drink that dictates the quality of your health.

To determine if your diet is balanced or not, look at your nutrition as a whole. Do the amount of fresh whole foods outweigh the amount of heavily-processed foods? Do your portion sizes align with your needs and goals? Do your food choices leave you feeling energized and content or tired and bloated?

There are thousands of ways to be healthy, and one of them can include wine and coffee, so if your tastebuds are anything like mine, I'd choose that way.

WHAT PARTS OF YOUR LIFE GOT BETTER WHILE YOU WERE DOING IT AND WHAT PARTS GOT HARDER?

Maybe as you lost weight, shopping for clothes got easier, and, in return, getting dressed to go out felt less like a hassle.

At the same time, it could have been mentally draining, difficult to focus and your entire weekend centered around *needing* to meal prep.

When you're in a relationship, you often feel a bit more "complete." The social pressure to date around or those awkward conversations at the Thanksgiving table about why you're not in a relationship yet are suddenly gone. Having a good partner means you have someone to hang out with, someone to adventure with and someone to confide in.

On the other hand, if it's an unhealthy relationship, it may cause more stress to say you need some alone time. And you may have difficulty sticking to your own schedule or being spontaneous with it because what once was a last-minute night out with friends, could turn into an argument of "Why didn't you tell me you weren't going to be home for the dinner I cooked beforehand?"

The longer you're in a relationship, the more effort each person needs to put in to keep it going. If you move in together, responsibilities like laundry, cooking, dishes and finances should get shared, but when they're not sorted out, this can cause strain on the relationship, filled with anxiety and resentment.

DID YOU LIKE THE PERSON YOU WERE WHEN YOU WERE IN IT/DOING IT?

Did you have anything to talk about other than what you eat and what workouts you do? Healthy eating and exercise are supposed to be *part* of your life, not all of it.

Is your partner in every story you tell? Was he/she all you spoke about?

Were you obsessed with thoughts of food that robbed your brain space from being occupied about other things like your job or friendships?

It's important to identify your passions. For example, if you love to dance, draw or play music and used to spend time doing those activities, but your diet or relationship pulls you away from them, it's clear something needs to change.

Your diet and relationship should inspire you to do more of what you love, not less of it.

WISDOM IS KNOWLEDGE APPLIED SO MISTAKES AREN'T REPEATED

There's an old proverb that states: "Fool me once, shame on you; fool me twice, shame on me." While this is usually about not being led astray by dishonest people, there is no one to whom this is more applicable than yourself.

Going through something once is a lesson. Going through the same thing twice is a mistake. After a third time, well, that's a pattern. Once you realize the pattern is there, you're no longer making a mistake, you're making a choice.

With both relationships and nutrition, so much of our early life is an experience of throwing ourselves into things with no regard for what lessons we might learn. We're in it for the moment, looking to get a short-term fix out of it.

But as we age, we've got to be more discerning because, whether we realize it or not, each of these experiences is showing us something about ourselves, about our bodies, about our hearts and minds. And it's up to us to learn, rather than simply stay in a cycle that doesn't suit us.

That's why self-examination is so important. Taking a step back after the fact to reflect and assess what you've learned is the very first step to learning what works for you.

In either case, to get there, you've got to develop skills. You need to go through a number of relationships (and diets) to determine not only what you want, but how to take that and incorporate it into the next phase of your life.

CHAPTER 10

PUTTING IT ALL TOGETHER

"People with goals succeed because
they know where they're going."

- Earl Nightingale, radio host and motivational speaker

In everything from business to sports, experts recommend looking at previous behaviors as a predictor of future performance.

This is true in our personal lives, too. If we know how we've behaved in regard to love and food, we should be able to predict how we will behave in the future, right?

That's a scary thought. If we believe it's true, we're accepting the idea that we can't change.

But, the truth is, your future isn't completely written in the stars. We *can* change our behaviors and the way we relate to them. All patterns can be broken.

You see, most of the time, people's repeated behaviors are subconscious. We tend to realize we're back in the same place only after we've arrived there. If we'd been more observant of how things were unfolding, we might have turned down a different path, which is why creating that awareness is the first step.

All of the exercises you've been given so far in this book serve two purposes: The first is to bring your bad habits to your attention while the second is to help you break free of them. Once you know how and why you make the same unhelpful choices repeatedly, you can move to the final step: Use that insight to form more helpful habits, leading to a brighter future.

In order to create an individualized nutrition plan, lifestyle or even romantic relationship, you need to start by looking at what actions breed success. For example, in relationships, it's often compatibility, communication and respect. With your diet, it's usually consistency, balance and flexibility. Using that information, you'll have all of the tools to design, from the ground up, exactly what you need.

I *assure you* that you *can* change because you've already started by reading this book. Now, you just need to build the roadmap that works best for your future self, which is precisely what you'll be doing in this chapter.

FIRST THINGS FIRST: WHAT'S NOT FOR YOU?

As I continue to learn more about myself, I look back at places where things didn't work out the way I'd planned. I think back to when I on-again-off-again dated a guy for nearly three years. Every time we would get back together, I'd tell him I was still interested in a committed relationship. He kept telling me he wasn't ready yet. I held on to that "yet" way too long.

He never gave me the insinuation he wanted something serious, but I wanted it so badly, I ignored his clear signs. Then I realized I was stuck in a pattern. I could wait until I was 40 when he might finally come around and may want to settle down. But I knew he wouldn't, and I was just wasting my time. That conclusion was incredibly useful to me, and now I encourage people to ask themselves some simple questions that can help them break their own cycles:

- If you had a few more tools at the time, could you have predicted (or perhaps avoided) the issues that came up in past relationships?
- With a bit more knowledge, would you have avoided the entire relationship?

If the answer to either of those questions is yes, that means you've learned something. Now, you can apply that lesson going forward to avoid any potential missteps.

Of course, even with clear communication, cultivated trust and shared vision, there are no guarantees of success in *any* relationship. But there *are* some reliable predictors of failure.

The most obvious of these is *incompatibility*. You have to recognize what absolutely does not work for you.

In relationships, we call them dealbreakers. All relationships take work, but it's helpful to get the true dealbreakers out of the way first.

It's important to agree on a few basic things:

- How do we handle disagreements?
- Do we both want monogamy?
- Are our values aligned?

In the end, it doesn't matter how good your communication or your chemistry or your sex life is, if you don't see eye-to-eye on the basics, it's hard to imagine things working out in the end.

The same is true for nutrition. Every one of my clients has a history of using diets that didn't work for them. I encourage them to look back at the places they struggled and do some deep auditing.

Why didn't it work? What were the real issues? What struggles were acceptable and which were simply insurmountable?

You've got to have a list of your dietary dealbreakers, too. You need to know with certainty what does *not* work for you and build a plan that doesn't rely on those things.

Now, while dealbreakers have to be addressed, they need to be reasonable. If you want to get fit but aren't open to exercising, then there's no logical way to build a plan around that.

Here's an example from my client Tiffany. During our initial consultation, I asked her about her previous attempts at weight loss. I encouraged her to focus on, what aspects of those plans she didn't like.

Here's what she said:

TIFFANY'S DEALBREAKERS

- I didn't like having to cook separate meals for myself and my family
- I didn't like how restrictive it was and the immense amount of guilt I felt for eating any type of sugar
- I didn't like that I had to workout for an hour every single day
- I didn't like that I had to track every macro
- I didn't like that I didn't know how to eat outside of tracking my intake

With that information, her dealbreakers became pretty clear: Anything that was overly complex or relied exclusively on rigid structure for it to be successful made her crazy. In the end, she couldn't thrive with that kind of constraint.

From there, we built a plan that took all of these dealbreakers into account. This allowed us to create something that made sense for her. For each of her particular dealbreakers, we found a way to sidestep the difficulty while still allowing for progress.

That chart below outlines what that looks like in practice.

TIFFANY'S DEALBREAKERS	FEATURES OF TIFFANY'S CUSTOMIZED PLAN
• Having to cook separate meals for herself and her family	• Recipes and methods to prepare nutritious meals she could enjoy with her family
• High level of food restriction led to guilt over eating any and all sugar	• We defined her version of moderation to make room for sweets without a side of guilt
• Daily workouts were too time consuming	• Restructured training schedule to allow for flexibility and built in rest days
• Over-reliance on tracking macronutrients	• Creation of staple meal and snack options to keep things simple without needing to track everything
• Lack of flexibility created uncertainty and anxiety when deviating from planned meals	• Practices to navigate social situations so she could build her plate in a balanced way without having it offset her progress

Now, let's figure out your dealbreakers.

In reviewing your dietary history, make a list of every diet or nutrition plan you've tried. By this stage of the book, you've probably got most of them at the front of your mind already.

For each of these, write down exactly what you didn't like about your diet. Focus on the aspects of the nutritional setup that made the diet hard to follow such as the things that affected your energy, your social life or your general sense of well being.

Some challenges are unavoidable, but if you think back, and you have some glaring memories of hating something, write it down.

Now, looking at those lists, see what comes up multiple times. If you had trouble going to bed hungry on several diets, that's a dealbreaker. If you found yourself overwhelmed by meal prep no matter how "simple" the plan said it would be, write that down. If you found yourself pushing through intestinal distress because of food sensitivities or allergies, note that.

These are your dealbreakers. You don't need to overcome them to be successful.

I promise you, it's very possible to lose weight and improve your health without spending every Sunday preparing meals for the week and packing them into neat little plastic containers. (But if you love doing that, you can!)

It's very possible to make progress with every aspect of your fitness without having to choke down protein shakes or supplements. (But if you enjoy them, you can!)

It's just as possible to lose weight and improve your health without tracking every bite of food that you put into your mouth. (But, if you enjoy doing that, guess what? Go ahead!)

The point is, your *dealbreakers* might be someone else's *dealmakers*. But, as we've covered several times so far, the goal is finding what works for you and building a plan around that.

Figuring out your right diet isn't about being Cinderella, just hoping someone comes along with a glass slipper that happens to fit. It's about being like Goldilocks: Trying everything and finding what's *just right* for you.

FOUNDATIONAL FUNDAMENTALS

Now that you're operating with a solid list of what you won't accept, it's time to dive into the things you absolutely need for a nutrition plan to work for you: Your must-haves. Think of your must-haves as the foundational level of what you're building for yourself. Without them, things quickly fall apart.

For example, in relationships, these would be trust, communication and attraction. Think of how relationships look when you remove one of those components. You *can* have a relationship without trust, or communication or attraction, but it'll probably end up pretty badly for those involved. The same goes with nutrition.

While every relationship looks different, and no two successful nutrition plans will be identical, there are some similar fundamentals.

In the case of dieting, when designing your own plan, you need to check a few universal boxes:

- You don't have to count calories, but calories *do* count. Eating in an energy deficit is required in order to lose weight, but how you manage that deficit is up to you
- Veggies don't need to be the *only* thing you eat, but they should be the star of the show
- Make protein present at every meal to keep your muscles strong. A palm-sized portion is great for most of us
- A balance of macros matter, but if you care about your health more than aesthetics, micronutrients matter most. The easiest way to get the diverse micronutrients you need is by eating an assortment of colorful fruits and veggies
- Eat omega-3 rich fats to support your heart and lubricate your joints. These can come from fish, avocados, nuts, seeds and some oils
- Carbohydrates are the most palatable food and therefore easiest to overeat, so while you don't need to avoid them completely, be mindful of your carb intake. Choose mainly complex carbohydrates like whole grains and starchy vegetables, as they carry fiber to help to regulate your bowels, reduce your likelihood of high cholesterol and monitor blood sugar
- It's OK to eat processed foods that come in a wrapper. With that said, if that's all you eat, you probably won't feel very well. As a general rule, try to eat more whole foods rather than processed foods

These tenants of a well-balanced diet and healthy eating should inform your decisions when you determine what your dealbreakers are so you can succeed.

SIGNS YOU'RE SETTLING IN YOUR RELATIONSHIP & DIET

RELATIONSHIP	DIET
• My partner only gets annoyed with me when I ask too many questions	• I only get hangry once a day
• He/she doesn't get along with any of my family or friends so I keep them separate	• The stress of trying to stick to my meal plan at a restaurant is too much, so I avoid going out with family and friends
• We used to be so happy and in love. It must be me I just need to work harder	• I used to be able to stick to this. It must be me. I just need to work harder
• At least we're not as bad as...(insert unhealthy relationship couple here)	• At least I can eat some carbs, unlike my co-worker who's miserable on Keto

CHAPTER 11

BECOMING GOLDILOCKS:
THE ONCE UPON A DIET METHOD

"There comes a day when you're going to look around
and realize happiness is where you are."

- *Moana,* strong willed Disney princess

If I had a dollar for every person that said: "Just tell me what to do," I'd be sitting pretty in a castle like the queen that I am.

Even though there are certain people who thrive in authoritarian coaching setups (doing exactly what they're told with little need for explanation), most of us live in a world where last-minute changes occur often. And, even without *needing* to make shifts based on circumstances, they tend to enjoy variety, especially in social situations.

That desire for flexibility requires the ability to choose foods that align with one's nutritional needs and not have those choices derail them. In other words, while many people *think* they want to be *told* what to do, what they really need is to be *taught* how to do it. Ever heard of the phrase: "Give a man a fish, and you feed him for a day; teach a man to fish, and you feed him for a lifetime?" That's where *The Once Upon a Diet Method* comes into play.

Implementing this method will help you sift through the overwhelming mixed messages surrounding you, figure out what makes sense for *you* and finally put an end to the obsessive thoughts around food. With this approach, it'll become clear what to eat, when to eat and how much to eat so you can stop Googling it.

Creating an individualized plan customized to your lifestyle habits will not only help you achieve your goals, you'll enjoy the process.

STEP 1: DETERMINE YOUR GOAL AND YOUR 'WHY'

Before anything else, you need to decide what you're actually trying to accomplish and why. The *why* is the most important part of this. When you clearly define your *why*, you are more likely to follow through. Then, when you feel stuck (because that's bound to happen), you can revisit your why, and that'll push you to stay motivated.

When you set about a journey into general wellness -- and, more specifically, health and fitness -- there are many areas you may be looking to improve.

As we've touched on earlier in this book, people tend to fixate on weight because it's what society tells us to focus on, and, it's quantifiable. We know where we stand when we look down at a scale to see if it's gone up or down.

But improving your health isn't as cut and dry as losing weight, so while weight loss is the most common goal for most of my clients, it's not the *only* goal, and it shouldn't be your *why*. Neither is it the end-all-be-all of a lifestyle overhaul, which is why I encourage them to look beyond the scale and set broader goals based on their behaviors and habits.

There are several goals you might be interested in achieving, all of which have different markers of health. A brief list of these includes, but is not limited to:

- Body composition
- Increased strength
- Improved mood
- How your clothes fit
- Digestive health
- Relationship with food
- Energy levels
- Overall well-being

Some of the above are related to the number we see on the scale, but many are more intangible. Increased strength could be determined by being able to lift heavier weights, but something like your relationship with food is harder to measure. In the case of more subjective goals, you need to pre-determine how you're going to measure progress, usually with some sort of rubric.

For example, while "digestive health" is fairly vague, it can be measured by noting improvements in bowel habits (more regular, less feeling of strain) or intestinal distress (less bloating). Increased energy might be measured in how easy it feels to get out of bed in the morning and how tired you feel at the end of a work day. In either case, you'll need to actually record these feelings. (To do this, refer back to the self-assessment chart in Chapter 6.)

One caveat here is while you should have one main goal to focus on, be *aware* of all the other goals. This will make it much more obvious you're actually making progress.

For instance, if weight loss is your goal, you might be looking at the scale every day. But if your *why* is increased strength, then you may be training with weights a few times a week. What you may not know is, as a general rule, early in a fitness program, strength will increase before you notice any weight loss.

But if you're only looking at the scale and not paying attention to the fact you're lifting more in the gym each week, you'd be completely unaware you're getting stronger. Being aware of your *why* gives you the full picture of what's changing while being unaware of it could lead to discouragement.

STEP 2: DETERMINE THE INTENSITY OF THE PLAN

Depending on your goal, you may need to have a more intense nutrition plan at first. And sometimes the best way to begin a marathon is with a sprint. And after that sprint ends, you are able to coast because that first burst of momentum is enough to keep you going.

Myself and many others I've coached have tried that sprint approach, and it didn't serve us well so we choose to maintain the same speed most of the time. There's an inverse relationship between length and intensity of a successful diet. The more intense it is, the shorter you'll want to follow it.

So, ask yourself: How intense do I want to be on a scale of one to five. One being "this barely feels like a change;" five being "I just turned my entire life upside down."

Typically, I recommend against a five. But, if you're at a four, that's a diet you can probably follow for six to 12 weeks before transitioning into something more sustainable.

On the other hand, if you don't want something as intense, and you feel like you're ready for a plan you can follow for the rest of your life, that's more like a two. What keeps many of my clients going past the honeymoon phase is realizing their tiny efforts build up over time and, with patience and consistency, they see big results.

Sometimes, you're ready to get married because you love the slow burn of a long-term partnership. Sometimes, you want a summer fling because it flares hot and fast and eventually fizzles. Both have their place, but you just need to know what you're looking for before getting into it.

STEP 3: DETERMINE YOUR METHOD OF TRACKING

You don't need to weigh every morsel of food, but you *do* have to have a general idea of what you're putting into your body.

You need to know how you want to manage things. Are you more of a micro-manager who wants to know all the details, or are you kind of laissez-faire and do better with a more relaxed system?

Here are a few options going from most rigid to more flexible:

- Count macros and micros
- Count macros
- Count calories and protein
- Count calories
- Measure food in portions - using a food scale/ measuring cups and spoons

- Measure food in portions - using your hand[26]
- Use the plate method for at least two meals per day (half non-starchy veggies, a fourth lean protein, a fourth whole grains)
- Keep a written food diary
- Take photos of your food
- Use mindful eating techniques - eat slower, honor your hunger and make nutritious swaps as you see fit

Often when I work with clients, I start from the least rigid and move toward the most rigid, stopping right before we get to the part of the list that feels too stressful to them. Remember, whatever your method, if it becomes more stressful than helpful, stop doing it.

The purpose of tracking isn't to do it the rest of your life (unless you genuinely like to). Instead, it's meant to bring awareness to your behaviors so you know what it is you need to change in order to be successful.

This is why working with a nutrition professional like a Registered Dietitian can be so powerful. They can see when it's time to encourage more tracking, encourage less tracking, modify the method of tracking, and tell you when you've built up enough healthy habits to stop doing it.

STEP 4: PRE-DETERMINE YOUR WINDOW OF OBSERVATION

Everything moves, but not everything moves at the same speed. As mentioned above, you'll often get stronger before you really begin seeing weight loss. For this reason, it's

---

[26] Using your hand as a way to measure portions is one of my favorite portion control methods because your hand is often proportionate to your body. For example: a toddler has a much smaller hand than an adult because their caloric needs are significantly lower as well. Use your fist to measure your grains/starches, your palm to measure your protein, and your thumb as a reference to measure your fats.

important to decide on a window of observation specific to your goal.

Some goals should be tracked daily like water and veggie intake, but some goals are up for debate. For example, studies show those who weigh themselves daily achieve better weight loss outcomes. With that said, this should be filtered through the lens of your personal relationship with the scale. If your goal is weight loss, and you understand the number on the scale is just data, and your mood isn't greatly affected by what you see, then weighing in each day may help you stay on track. But if weighing yourself every morning is triggering to you, and the number starts dictating how you go about the rest of your day, this is not a helpful method for you.

Other goals have to be tracked less frequently. To see real change in your temperament, energy levels or sleep habits, you'd need to look at the aggregate data over the course of a month. And, for things like how many minutes you're moving each day, it's best to track your weekly averages.

Either way, pick the right window for your goal, and stick to it.

STEP 5: DETERMINE HOW OFTEN YOU'RE GOING TO EAT OUT

You need to establish that, whether you're dining out or ordering in, meals prepared at restaurants are in an entirely different category than meals you prepare yourself, even pre-packaged meals.

Restaurants are in the business of making their food taste as good as possible, which often means adding extra butter, oils, salt and sugary sauces. And, to boot, the portions are much larger. Even if you use the plate method, the caloric content of these meals is much higher than you'd imagine.

I'm not saying this to scare you away from eating out. It just means that, because these meals are prepared differently, you need to take that into account.

Depending on where you are in life, how often you order in or dine out will vary. For example, if you're single, and your idea of a good time is going to a bar or club to drink and dance, then factoring in those potential late-night activities is going to be important to you, and you'll need to learn how to handle it mindfully. And that's OK. The key is to learn how to find balance.

STEP 6: DETERMINE YOUR PLAN FOR UNFORESEEN EVENTS

What will you do when your group of friends votes against the healthy restaurant you were hoping they'd pick? Or when your groceries don't get delivered in time for you to do your weekly meal prep? How about when the new person you're crushing on wants to take you to the ice cream spot that just opened up?

You can have the best intentions in the world and still need to pivot. You wake up late and skip breakfast; you accidentally leave your packed lunch at home; you thought you ordered enough vegetables to last you a week but run out after two days; you get caught up at a social event and end up overeating. All of these examples *can* and *will* happen. Just because a curveball was thrown your way last-minute doesn't mean you have to wait to "start over."

Instead of freaking out and deciding nothing is worth doing if it can't be done at 100%, try putting forth an 80% effort. Expect unforeseen events (that's life!), and choose to have a figure-it-out attitude. Make the best of the situation by focusing on the overall effort you're putting in instead of trying to be perfect all the time.

STEP 7: DETERMINE HOW YOU ARE GOING TO DEAL WITH MISTAKES

You will slip up, but don't give up. Know this: Old habits die hard. It's human nature to choose what feels familiar or safe, which is why creating new habits can feel uncomfortable. This is where the old habits start to creep back in, and it's at that point where you'll need to push past the discomfort in order to create sustainable change.

You also won't always feel motivated. That's when you need to remember your *why*. Why did you start working toward this goal in the first place? Why is this important to you? What's one thing you can do to draw closer to achieving this goal, even when it feels so far away?

The sooner you get back to doing what makes you feel good, the closer you'll be to achieving whatever you want to.

So instead of giving up:

- Learn to be flexible and make the best of all situations, especially when circumstances aren't "perfect"
- Explore how to manage situations outside of your control like ordering takeout, social events, holidays and a hectic schedule
- Be patient and figure out what works for *you*

Because this I know for sure: Giving up won't get you to your goal any faster.

HERE'S HOW YOU CAN USE THE ONCE UPON A DIET METHOD THE 'INTENSE' WAY:

Barbara wants to lose 18 pounds. Having used the steps above, she's ready to design a plan that will allow her to do that and keep it off for good. That starts with some self-assessment.

Before anything else, she needs to know where she's starting, so for two weeks leading up to her plan, Barbara begins recording her food intake. Looking at that information, she sees she's been averaging between 2,200 and 3,100 calories per day. That's a big range, but her food log makes the culprit very obvious: Alcohol. On days she doesn't drink, Barbara averages 2,000 to 2,300 calories. On days she does drink, it's 2,900 to 3,300. Not only does she get the extra calories from the alcohol, but she also winds up eating more, too.

Now, Barbara needs to determine the intensity of her plan -- and she does this by really looking at what's worked for her in the past *and* what's created issues. She knows from her experiences she gets really excited about when she first starts any new plan. But after those first few weeks, if things feel too hard, she eventually loses steam.

With that information, Barbara decides she is willing to use a pretty intense "jump start" type of plan, and then transition into something more moderate. For some people, this could be a mistake. But Barbara's history with dieting has given her insight into her own habits and psychology, and she feels confident she can translate her motivation into long-term habits.

In designing her plan, she decides she'll aim for 1,500 calories per day[27]. To achieve this, she's going to eliminate alcohol completely for 30 days. With that change alone, she'll be bringing her average caloric intake into the 2,000 to 2,300 range. To achieve the rest of the deficit, she'll reduce her food intake.

Barbara also decides she's going to measure her food for the first 60 days to build the habit. She doesn't want to count *all* of her macros because she also knows the beginning of a new plan can be quite overwhelming. She feels more comfortable tracking her protein and calories. To help her stick to the plan, she'll incorporate the plate method at lunch and dinner and make sure to start her day with at least 20 grams of protein.

At this point, her plan seems very reasonable. Just by doing these simple things, she'll be able to maintain a deficit while getting enough protein to allow for both satiety and recovery.

From here, Barbara needs to plan for weekends. Since Friday's dinner is pizza night with the kids, she will account for two slices and a garden salad. She also knows on Sundays the family likes to bake her favorite: Cookies. So she will plan to enjoy three cookies with a glass of milk once a week. All of these are taken into account and tallied up in terms of her daily and weekly caloric allotment. So *even though* Barbara has decided on an "intense" plan to start, she isn't feeling completely restricted.

At special occasions, restaurants or work events, she will make her best educated guess about the foods that seem harder to track because she understands tracking is a tool to help her stay accountable to her plan. Tracking is not *the plan*.

---

[27] Working with a RD can determine a healthy caloric intake for you based on your height, weight, sex, activity level, and goals.

When she wants to eat more, she identifies whether her craving is physical or emotional. She starts by assessing how active she was, the quality of her food, how much sleep she got and her stress level. Using that data, she'll either choose to eat more or not. Either way, she knows one day going over her calories won't take her out of the deficit, but a week of it will.

At the end of the eight weeks, Barbara expects to have lost around nine pounds, which means she'll be halfway to her goal. At that point, she'll transition to something more reasonable, including a daily energy intake of 1,800 calories. She'll also stop tracking calories but keep tracking protein. This will be slower, and she expects to be following this moderate plan for 16 weeks, and, hopefully, beyond that.

HERE'S HOW YOU CAN USE THE ONCE UPON A DIET METHOD THE "LESS INTENSE" WAY:

Gina is done with counting points, tracking macros and weighing everything she wants before she eats it. She's accepted the fact that, although those methods have helped her lose weight quickly in the past, she always gains it back. She's identified a pattern of doing things "perfectly" until she burns out, slipping back into her old ways, convincing herself

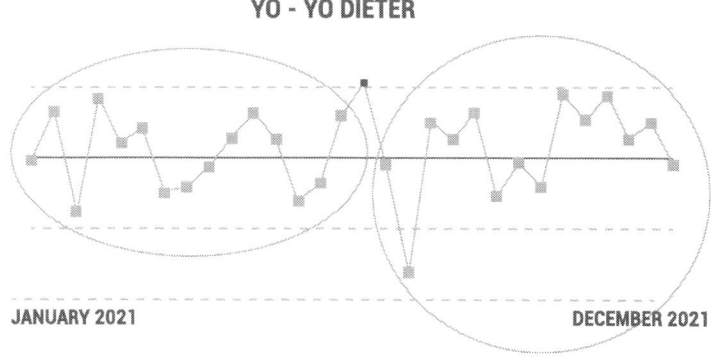

YO - YO DIETER

JANUARY 2021   DECEMBER 2021

SLOW & STEADY

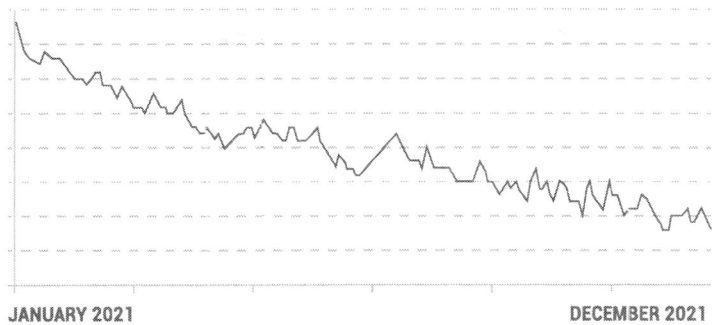

JANUARY 2021   DECEMBER 2021

she'll never lose the weight she wants, so why even try?
The majority of people who come to me resonate with Gina.
They want to lose weight but are tired of the extreme and
drastic changes required to change overnight. They try too
much, too quickly and their motivation fizzles out before
they can reap the benefits of their hard work.

It's at this point I explain to them they're not always going
to feel motivated, which is why we need to create habits and
behaviors that begin to feel like second nature. But that takes
time. Staying motivated requires accomplishing small wins
consistently over time. So we start with the lowest hanging
fruit -- the one thing she doesn't feel is too hard. Often it's as
simple as drinking more water or adding more vegetables to
the dinner plate. From there, we add on.

Before you know it, Gina is eating balanced meals, honoring
her cravings without going overboard, engaging in the
regular physical activity she enjoys and navigating social
situations with confidence.

With this approach, my clients need to understand every
week won't be a weight loss week. Most of the time, they'll

lose a half a pound to a pound or so. But some weeks, their weight may even go up. Then, I explain to them why they can't quit when the scale doesn't appear to reflect the effort they put in:

- The scale varies day-to-day, and a pound could be the difference of a bowel movement, a good night's sleep, some salty food, a late-night meal or the phase of your menstrual cycle
- Giving up won't make it come off faster. Consistency is *everything*. Stopping now will only lead to more weight gain, bringing you right back where you started (wanting to lose weight and make a change)
- The scale is not the most effective way to measure success. Focus on your actions and how you feel. Do you feel good? Do you have more energy? Did you follow through on what you said you were going to do?

Weight loss is a tricky thing and can easily make you lose sight of the long-term goal, which should be to feel happy, healthy, confident and proud of yourself. Don't let an arbitrary number on the scale rob you of that.

CONCLUSION

"Finding true love is like finding the missing piece to your puzzle. Once you discover it, the picture starts to look a lot clearer."

- Unknown

After reading this book, I hope you understand there are many ways to be happy *and* healthy. Neither of which depend on a number on a scale, but both of which can be achieved using *The Once Upon A Diet Method.*

You don't have to cut out sugar or exclude your favorite foods like pasta or pizza, but, like we established in chapter 7, if you never define what moderation means to you, you'll have trouble reaching your goals.

Remember, depriving yourself doesn't feel good and overindulging doesn't either.

To break the diet cycle and find balance in your eating habits, you'll need to experiment with finding your happy medium. Like I've discussed in this book, here are some things you can implement to be successful in your journey:

- Instead of focusing on how foods are going to make you *look*, focus on how foods are going to make you *feel*. This will almost always lead you to make better choices

- Instead of sticking to strict "all-or-nothing" concepts, practice being selective. Pause to think of what you truly want to eat before engaging. Ask yourself: "How will this make me feel now and how will it make me feel in a few hours?"
- Remove (insert "bad" food item here) from the pedestal. If you feel like you have to earn it to deserve it, you're more likely to fall into harmful behaviors like extreme restriction or excessive exercise, which always backfires
- If you're not seeing the progress that you want, replace the idea of *disappointment* with *data* so you can make better and more informed choices going forward
- Create an environment to thrive. For example: Keep healthier options on hand so they're easily accessible
- Rather than depending on when you *feel* like working out, schedule when you'll get your daily movement in
- Get quality sleep, consistently, and if sleep doesn't come easily to you then make resting a priority
- Fuel your body with three balanced meals per day and snack when you need to
- Engage in healthy stress management techniques like meditating or journaling
- Join a support group of people who are working towards breaking up with diets, too (Shameless plug: Join the "Healthy Lifestyle Support With Toni" group on Facebook)

Creating the best diet that works for you takes patience and self-awareness, just like finding the perfect mate.

In both nutrition and relationships, if it's gonna work, it has to be the right fit. At the same time, trying to make something fit when it clearly doesn't hasn't worked for anyone.

We're not Cinderella. We won't have Prince Charming knocking on our door holding the perfect glass slipper. It's more realistic than that. That's why you've gotta get your Goldilocks on.

The truth is: If you want to find a diet that really works for you, both now and in the future, you've got to date around.

You have to learn what you don't want to figure out what you do want. For most of us, that means a bunch of bad dates, dramatic relationships and a few painful breakups. It also means ups and downs on the scale, fancy cookbooks we stop using and low-calorie meals we hate.

You may feel disappointed to learn there's no magic solution to weight loss or Cupid coming to find you your partner. I know I was.

But what I had to spend years learning so you don't have to waste any more time is this: Nothing (and no one) is perfect but that doesn't mean you have to settle for less.

Whether it's a date or a diet, the chances of finding anything that immediately works perfectly are pretty slim. It's never a waste of your time if you learn something from it. So don't just finish this book and say "I read it" and forget about it. I want you to say "I'm doing it" instead. I want you to use this as a workbook and implement one tip from the book at a time. Once one tip becomes a habit, come back to your handy dandy book and implement another thing.

Continue to work at this and soon enough you'll be eating healthy (consistently) and feeling like the best version of yourself, not just for a week, not just for a month, but for a lifetime.

If you do these things, I assure you *The Once Upon A Diet Method* will bring you closer to *your happy beginning.*

Made in the USA
Las Vegas, NV
01 April 2022